Driving by Memory

Driving by Memory

William Fox

University of New Mexico Press Albuquerque

Library of Congress Cataloging-in-Publication Data

Fox, William L., 1949–

Driving by memory / William L. Fox. — 1st ed.

p.   cm.

Includes bibliographical references (p.   ).

ISBN 0-8263-1944-0. — ISBN 0-8263-1945-9 (pbk.)

1. Las Vegas (Nev.)—Description and travel.   2. Fox, William L.,
1949–   —Journeys—Nevada—Las Vegas.   3. Fox, William L., 1949–
—Journeys—West (W.S.)   4. West (U.S.)—Description and travel.
5. Nevada—Description and travel.   6. Automobile travel—West
(U.S.)   7. Automobile travel—Nevada.   I. Title.

F849.L35F69   1999

917.804′33—dc21   98-40560

                                                              CIP

Acknowledgments

Patrick McFarlin, Joseph Guglietti, Frank Rollo, and the PDC of Santa Fe—
for the righteous encouragment of one's peers without which little is
accomplished.

Jeff Kelley—for defining the difference between site and place, and Kirk
Robertson—for writing the poems in *Driving to Las Vegas*.

David Abel and Kathy Kuehn—just because.

Robert and Polly Beckmann—for welcoming me at the end of each trip with
conversation and clean sheets.

Tom Radko—for reading and editing almost every word for eight years.

Beth Hadas—for encouraging these essays from the very start.

Dana Asbury—for shepherding the book into print.

Beth Bradley Fox—for being the smart, strong, and loving partner of a lifetime, and for counting.

And all the residents of all the towns through which these travels pass—
whose stories and lives are complicated far beyond my telling.

Contents

Retro Sublime

My mother's red hair stands up slightly, as if electrified and combed from the wrong side, and she won't look at me during the whispered consultation with my grandparents. Out front on Las Palmas Street, the long black Cadillac that brought her down from Santa Barbara idles, the driver smoking in the front seat. I'm nine years old and this Christmas is making less and less sense to me. I've been packed off from home without any explanation to spend the holidays with my grandparents in Los Angeles, in a house where I've never so much as spent the night before. And once here, I've been treated like an invalid, as if I'd been subjected to a debilitating bout of the flu. Even my grandmother's friends keep asking me if I'm all right.

The three adults are solemnly nodding now, and Grandmother begins to pack up both my clothes and new presents. Mom asks me if I want to go on a trip, and of course I say: *Sure.* It's the night before New Year's Eve, and what better way to bring in 1959 than driving off through the night inside such an immense automobile.

The driver opens the rear doors for us, and we climb into the longest leather seat I've ever seen, even larger than my father's reading chair. Heading north on Highland Avenue, then passing through the Hollywood Hills and into the San Fernando Valley, I fall asleep. Sometime after midnight my mother zombie-walks me into a motel room, tucks me into one bed and herself into the other.

We get a late start the next morning after breakfast in a nearby coffeeshop, and it takes us all day to drive up the Central Valley of California and pick up Highway 50 heading east into the mountains. By the time we reach Echo Summit, the pine trees on either side of the road are black, but in the full moon the ground looks white. I can't tell if it's the moonlight or snow, but hope it's the latter; I've never seen snow before, and it is, after all, Christmas vacation. I doze until we're down from the pass and the driver says quietly:

There's Lake Tahoe. The water is dark, sand beaches glowing—snow on sand in moonlight, I decide. Small cabins are set back from the road, and the sarcophagus shapes of gas pumps stand guard before closed filling stations.

Mother is smoking a cigarette pensively in the front seat, and I'm about to stretch out again in the back when there's a distinct change in the scenery. There's more light around us, the night air almost pink. Motels now line the road, all with "No Vacancy" signs lit in red neon. People are out walking arm in arm on both sides of the street, laughing and carrying open champagne bottles. The tires sound different on the pavement, rougher and arhythmic, the highway suddenly paved more crudely. It's as if we've been time-warped forward out of some sleepy 1920's mountain town into an amusement park for grownups. We're immersed in the neon glow just long enough for me to grasp that the driver is telling us we've crossed into Nevada. The pink haze may be two blocks long in all, and then we're through it, the lights now hidden by forest.

The Cadillac begins a slow climb over Spooner Summit, the final mountain pass, trees dropping away in front of us as we crest the rim of the Tahoe Basin and then descend into what looks like the moon itself, ghostly white hills where granite outcroppings replace the trees. At the bottom of the pass we turn left and a few minutes later are surrounded by the eye-popping neon of Carson City. With the signs blinking in a gathering snowstorm, we make another late check-in, this time to a Travelodge. There's a green sign out front with a bear in a nightshirt sleepwalking, paws outstretched. He's in a waking dream and I know how he feels.

It's snowing lightly when I wake up the next morning, and first thing I go out for a walk with the driver, whose name is Jim. The air is the coldest I've ever felt, the landscape the most barren imaginable. There are several things here to establish for myself as we search for breakfast on the first day of the year. First, even at nine years old, there's only one reason I can imagine being dragged into the middle of a small Nevada town crouched amongst the snow-covered bushes that I take to be sagebrush: Divorce. It's one of the two forbidden words I know, the other being "the Big C," cancer, which I reject as a likely explanation, there being no hospital in sight. Jim maintains a respectful silence when I ask him if he knows why we're here.

Somehow, though, our encampment in this very alien landscape, one that looks to me like a science fiction movie set on Mars, makes that unuttered word much more acceptable. The tiny capital of Nevada resonates slightly this morning with the air of an illicit friction, the same way the border at Tahoe did last night, and there's an unnatural amount of energy on the street for a place this desolate, even on New Year's Day. Already, just eight hours into the Great Basin, it's obvious that there are distinctions to be made between here, Nevada, and everywhere else. When Mother gets up, closer to lunch than breakfast, her hair has calmed down. Whatever it is we're here to do, it's apparently acceptable once you get over the mountains and into the desert.

TWO

I spent much of our six weeks at the Washoe Pines divorce ranch on a horse, first riding out alone onto the winter fields of Washoe Valley and down to the shoreline of its shallow lake. I learned how to cross barbed wire fences and avoid the territorial imperative of the two bulls pastured between the ranch and the highway, and then how to negotiate Nevada's traffic, which was not yet subject to a national speed limit. Out in the valley, old wooden barns were burnished to a low silver by the winter sun, and the ruins of stone buildings were surrounded by half-buried heaps of rust.

Although the highest ridges between Lake Tahoe and Washoe Valley were deep in snow, the foothills up and into nearby Little Valley were accessible, and as I got used to being alone on a horse, I rode up into the mountains. I surprised deer and beaver on my rides, stumbled across arrowheads in the sandy banks by the creek, and once found a mountain lion calmly observing me from atop granite boulder across the valley. I was thrilled to have crossed the barriers of my imagination, to have entered that secret and dangerous desert I knew would exist beyond my childhood. I cherished the solitude. Riding back to the ranch in the cold shadows of January afternoons, I would marvel that it took a divorce to get me here.

The rest of the time I attended a fifth grade class in Carson City, where the most useful lessons came from my fellow students. They taught me how to play marbles as we knelt in the rough decomposed rock that passed for sand in the schoolyard, and how to place bets on the outcome. My mother got drunk, flirted with the cowboys, and caught pneumonia. Her friend Margaret, who came up from Los Angeles to care for the two of us, gave me a Kodak Brownie camera, and although none of my first photographs remain, I re-member looking through its viewfinder and realizing how framing a view, cutting out part of reality, was the way a story was told. Margaret also taught me how to play solitaire, hearts, and the double-deck game of canasta, though much to my disappointment she wouldn't accept wagers.

While I don't remember what presents I was given at my grandparents' that Christmas, I regard the drive itself as a gift of the first magnitude. The trip to Nevada was my first to last more than a day and to cross a state line. It is the baseline from which I measure my life, a story arcing between land and mem-ory that established what was past and what present, what was there and now here. How I perceived time as a boy and what it means to me now remain a matter of where I am in relation to that baseline, the coming into the Great Basin, the terrain of my memory landscaped ever since by driving through the desert.

And it was a journey, literally, into the direction I had longed for ever since I was old enough to look out the window in my childhood bedroom. Almost every day until we moved to Santa Barbara I would perch at that window and stare north-by-northeast from our house above La Jolla. The Pacific Ocean framed the entire view to the left, and blocking my vision on the other hand was the hillside, but in front of me and over the low coastal hills was open sky. On the corresponding page in an atlas, which rested open upon my table, nothing was shown in that direction but emptiness. Blue sky out my window and white paper on a map, the blank page of adventure.

The move from La Jolla up the coast to Santa Barbara the previous year, when I was eight, had at least been a step to the north. And the view out to sea had been considerably enhanced by the offshore presence of the Channel Islands, over which lightning sometimes played as my father stood with me on the terrace to watch. But none of it could compete with that inland mystery I had first imagined as starting just beyond the hills north of Miramar Naval Air Station when we lived in La Jolla, and then over the Santa Ynez Mountains just across the street from our place in Santa Barbara. Now I was actually in the desert, over the mountains and across all of California, and in the cold and empty map of my imagination.

After the requisite six-week Nevada residency, and only fifteen minutes in the Washoe County Courthouse in Reno, we returned to Santa Barbara, the house in Montecito, the ocean views. My father had moved out already, and within a few months, less than a year after our initial shift from La Jolla, so did we. I was sent off once again, this time for the summer to a camp in the high southern Sierra where I learned to hike and fish with four dozen other boys. In August on the last day of camp I was surprised to see Jim pull up in the big Cadillac. He set my duffel bag in the trunk, this time opening the front passenger door for me, an acknowledgment that we were, after all, friends with a shared history. As we drove slowly down to the highway he informed me that our destination was Reno, where my mother had moved a few weeks earlier. Beyond that he had few details to offer, assuming his customary reticence. I froze up inside. Visiting the desert was fine, but leaving the ocean behind? Forever?

Although it might have been logical to cross the Sierra to the east and drive

nat secret and dangerous desert I knew would exist beyond my childhood.

north on US 395, we didn't. Instead, we drove again down to the Central Valley, where the heat was relieved by several chocolate milkshakes along the way. Once more we motored through Tahoe on Highway 50, but this time during the day, and I remember the pleasure at recognizing billboards for Harold's Club in Carson City, signs that had been there in December, and that now pointed the way to my new home.

THREE

It was shockingly brown in Nevada that fall, especially after the tall pines and fern grottoes of Sequoia National Forest. By October, though, I had found a bike route that took me up to the edge of the city after school, a place where streets ended in the foothills of the Sierra. You could look east and north across the valley of the Truckee Meadows to where the fields ran out into desert and the high dry ranges of the Great Basin. I stared so long that my eyes watered. The mountain shadows crept over the town, neon from the casinos downtown replacing daylight, and the full hunter's moon rose so close I thought I could almost walk out onto it, its face a perfect reflection of the dusty Great Basin below. I surveyed my past, my present, my future, thinking I would never leave Nevada.

Santa Fe to Las Vegas

Selected Overpasses

It's 7 A.M. on Sunday morning December 3, the sun still behind Atalaya Mountain just east of Santa Fe, and it looks to be another cloudless day in this unending autumn. I pass only a few cars along St. Francis Drive as I head over to the interstate, everyone with their lights still on, and mark off my first abandoned car, a dejected primer-coated Pontiac Bonneville parked by the entry ramp, another victim of the weekend. Once on the freeway I set the cruise control at 75 mph, unlace and slip off my shoes, then lean back to enjoy the light as it spreads across the Rio Grande and the Jemez Mountains.

I'm almost fifteen minutes southbound out of town on I-25 before I realize that, somewhere along this trip to Las Vegas and back, I'm going to pass a lifetime milestone. I've been driving since the summer of 1966 and now, late in 1995, twenty-nine years later, I'm going to go over my first million miles in a car. My fifteenth car, to be exact, a dark blue 1991 Honda Civic four-door with AM-FM and no air-conditioning. Grow up driving a VW bug throughout the state of Nevada in the days when there was no speed limit, and you figure open windows will just take care of it. Hard habit to get over, especially the more expensive gasoline and the more fragile the ozone layer become. I roll under the first overpass of the trip, Exit #248, clearance of 16'10". Medium-height, I guess you could call it. Two more empty vehicles sit by the side of the freeway, a trailer of some kind with metal lattice sides and a late model Ford sedan. How do I know when I'm going to pass a million miles? Simple: by counting, though of an oddly imprecise variety.

It's not as if there's an odometer reeling off mileage behind my sunglasses, nor am I an especially compulsive counter—though I do keep track of how many cars are pulled off between Santa Fe and Albuquerque every time I make the drive. There's not another stretch of road quite like it in America for the sheer density of broken, stalled out, stolen, crashed, rolled, burned, and just plain left-and-walked-away-from automobiles. I don't know the statistical breakout of the causes, though many of them are neglected American sedans from the mid-1970s. Age might have something to do with it but, to be fair, there's usually a smattering of late-model pickups, Nissans, and the occasional minivan as well. Only one Honda in the last two years, however. I've already started the count for today with the Bonneville, the Ford, and the trailer, knowing that this particular tally will be kept only while I'm in the Rio Grande Valley—after that the rate drops off to such a low level as to be uninteresting.

Overpass number two, Exit #165 to Rio Rancho, 17'5", a tall one. Red and white Chevy pickup parked underneath, fourth victim, no one around. James McMurtry's on the radio with a new song, perfectly appropriate given both his and his dad's proclivity for driving. Larry McMurtry at one time had a reputation for frequently driving a convertible Cadillac cross-country on a marathon schedule. Seems like a perfectly natural mode of meditation, especially for a novelist from Texas who owns a bookstore in Georgetown (which features the most massive collection of mid-century American detective novels complete with dust jackets of anywhere I know). Road trips are a perfect time to consolidate one's skill at weaving trivia into a seamless web that almost appears to make sense. It's a remnant of our archaic oral history tradi-

Road trips are a perfect time to consolidate one's skill at weaving trivia

tion, this restringing of random remembrances into narrative so we don't lose our place in the scheme of things. Homer would be proud.

I know I'm going to pass a million miles because I keep rough track of how many miles I've driven on each of the cars I've owned: only 15,000 on that first VW bug—then almost 80,000 on the MG-B roadster that followed—75,000 on the green Volvo commuting back and forth from college in southern California to Reno—under 5,000 on the 1952 Riley in New Zealand—35,000 on the mid-engine Porsche. . . . There are a few high-mileage cars in there, one a VW fastback when I was driving from Reno to Santa Cruz on a regular basis to print books at Kayak Press with George Hitchcock and Raymond Carver. And three or four different vans, sedans, and a Jeep CJ-7 driven all up and down the Sierra with my rock-climbing partners looking for virgin vertical territory.

Anyway, a million, sometime within the approximately 1,400 miles I'll drive on this trip. It's 7:50 A.M. and I decide I'll count every overpass, something I've been wanting to do each time I make this drive, usually twice a year. In fact, I think I'll count all sorts of things to memorialize the occasion in a blizzard of quantification, another kind of narrative to mark my place. Interstate freeways are designed to be generic, to elude specificity, to be therefore absolutely predictable in their facilitation of transport, whether for military vehicles in the Cold War paranoia of the 1950s, when these roads were designed, or nowadays for consumer goods, another matter of strategic interest to capitalism. The interstates were designed to resist attention, to be a transparent part of the landscape, and it will be a challenge to see if I can examine the environment of the road itself.

In addition to commemorating my millionth mile by resisting this scenic manipulation, I have another motive for the counting mania: I'm curious

to a seamless web that almost appears to make sense.

about how we move through terrain from point to point, tracing a line on foot or by car, and constructing a mental picture of land, an analog, a "landscape"—and how that fits into the art of the region. That's the tax-deductible part of the trip, going to Las Vegas to interview Rita Deanin Abbey, who's an "abstract landscape" painter. I've been writing about artists working in the region, and have been led toward a distinction between land and landscape, between the actual ground we walk or drive on, and our mental picture of it. Given that the road is now inescapably part of the American landscape—how else could anyone negotiate a million miles of surface travel?—it looks as if I need to include it as part of the picture, so to speak. It's not that I'll solve an intellectual mystery by counting radio stations and road kill, but it will focus what has become for me a long inquiry into how our perceptions of art and land influence each other.

I pass my first cop of the day, a New Mexico highway patrolman who's parked predictably just on the outskirts of Albuquerque. We ignore each other, mostly because it's one of the few times I'll actually be even close to the speed limit today. Another reason for commemoration is President Clinton's recent signing of the annual Department of Transportation appropriation bill, which this year carries a Republican rider eliminating the federal speed limit on December 8. So, for the first time in recent memory, the states I'm passing through—New Mexico, Arizona, Nevada—will soon be raising their speed limits above 65 mph. Most seem slated to post 75 on at least the interstates, the original speed for which these roads were designed. The speed limit for trucks will also be raised, jumping from 55 to 65 in most states; given that truckers make their wages by the hour, that's going to give some of them as much as a 17 percent pay hike. Montana's even reverting to the great wide-open on rural roads during daylight hours, and for a moment I ponder the attraction. I bear right onto I-40 westbound, pass the fifth abandoned car of the morning, a Pinto station wagon so faded I can't tell what color it is, cross the Rio Grande, and start the long climb up out of the valley.

The next overpass is 16′0″. No height at all. A compact sedan with Arizona license plates goes zooming under it and down the grade on the other side of the median, passing all the semi-trailer trucks. Bad idea. As soon as you turn onto I-40, you're in one of the great east-west vehicular arterials of America which pumps goods twenty-four hours a day all along its 2,400 miles from Durham, North Carolina, to Barstow, California. On this road the trucks rule; their ratio with cars may vary, from 1:2 to the opposite, 2:1, but they always outgun anything else in tonnage. How fast they run is usually how fast it's safe to go.

Directly behind me the Sandia Mountains shimmer in a dry blue haze, just as bereft of snow as the Sangre de Cristo Mountains outside of Santa Fe. It's been an almost completely dry fall throughout the physiographic province of the Colorado Plateau, temperatures running fifteen degrees above normal week after week. Even Mt. Baldy, the highest peak near Santa Fe at 12,622 feet, is brown on its south face all the way to the summit. The next big mountain I'll pass will be Mt. Taylor, one of the four sacred Navajo mountains, which rises behind the small city of Grants. Its blasted-out volcanic summit tops out at 11,301, and I'm wondering if it, too, is dry. It occurs to me that this memory of records and averages, of what temperature and precipitation are supposed to be and extremes they've reached, has to do with my definition of and relationship to land. Not landscape: I'm not talking about what the picture is supposed to look like, but how cold and wet it's going to be when I hike somewhere.

No time to ponder the point, given the white patrol car that's now coming up behind me, three cars back. I'm going with the flow, but that's close to 75 mph in what is still a 65 zone; the speed limit signs won't be changed for several weeks. The last ticket I got in New Mexico was for doing 75 on the interstate, the same as everyone else; we were just a car targeted at random out of the traffic, and my "flow" argument didn't appear to faze the patrolman. Exit #149, 16′2″, and the cop uses it to go up and over the freeway, turning back with lights on, presumably to chase the speeding sedan from Arizona. I pass the "Shooting Range—State Park" sign as we crest the western rim of the Rio Grande Valley, and then I'm on the first real downhill. A black Kenworth eighteen-wheeler from Missouri comes up from behind, pauses, then eases out from behind me at 76 mph. Things in general are speeding up now that we're out of the valley—no more cars are pulled off, and the six I counted make an absolute record for the minimum. Must be because it's Sunday. The radio announces it's going to reach a high of 60 degrees from here to near anywhere else I could drive in a day.

TWO

It's 8:15, about a dozen semis in view, everyone moving along close to 80 mph. Exit #131, overpass at 16′10″. The first train of the day passes going east. It's a Santa Fe Railroad string with three engines and nearly a hundred flat cars, each with a container aboard. Exit #126, 16′8″. At 8:29 A.M. another train, this one with four engines and about seventy-five flat cars with two semi-trailers stacked on each. Hard to count the cars when the trains are going east and our combined speed is about 140 mph. Trains in the West have a very different appearance in the landscape from those elsewhere; out here you can often see the whole thing all at once, a sentence played out parallel to the road across the desert. The trains are either silvery containers or rust red freight cars; either way, they're not of the land, but on it, part of our picture of it, thus part of the landscape. Exit #102, and I take it, coast down to the bottom, and turn left to the rest stop. This is an exit for Acoma and Sky City, one of the most magnificent pueblos in New Mexico, so the rest stop is busy. The third train goes by at 8:43 A.M., and the fourth at 8:58 while I'm taking a restroom break. Keeping track is more work than I expected, given that there's a train coming by at just under every quarter of an hour. Back in the Honda, I arrange a half bagel in my lap and some apple juice in the dashboard cup holder, then ease up onto the freeway again, inserting myself into a line of trucks. The air is unstable in the extreme, the lightweight Honda handling well but a little shaky in the turbulent wake of six semis. That's 108 large wheels kicking up an unpredictable amount of backwashing air, and I break out left and around the trucks into calm air before attempting breakfast.

Just east of Grants the road cuts through the northern edge of the Malpais lava beds, the flows lying in small valleys among buff-colored sandstone-capped mesas. Little mesas, big lava beds. Supposed to be good hiking, and as I always do when passing through here, I get a little resentful. It's hard for me to choose between passing through in a hurry to get where I'm going and taking the time to get out and walk around—the choice between experiencing this terrain as landscape, a succession of pictures outside my window, or as land, a continuous and tactile insertion of myself while hiking. I suppose I might consider the ideal to be a combination of chances to do both, considering how much I enjoy traveling through country I've hiked—except life's too short. There's too much land that's too interesting and not enough time to hike it all. Maybe that's a greed fueled at least in part by the act of driving—of seeing more land than we otherwise could, and lusting to explore it, to be in and part of it, not passing by and apart. I ruminate about the connection between the television screen and the windshield, about our indoctrination by advertising into a state of constant consumption. Do I consider the land I see through the windshield to be advertised, to be transformed into merely landscape and therefore simply consumable, yet one more commodity?

We come up out of the lava beds and there's Mt. Taylor. Dry. Well, at least that's a peak I've been on, though driven off by 60 mph–plus winds a year ago. There wasn't much snow then, either, but a few inches had consolidated all around the peak at about the 10,500-foot level. God, that was a frigid hike before my wife, Beth, and I turned back to regain the cover of the trees. Although windy, the sky had been clear; cupping our eyes to prevent them from tearing up, we could trace the Sangre de Cristos 120 miles to the north, the Sandias 60 miles east, and Humphrey's Peak above Flagstaff, Arizona's highest point over 200 miles west.

We stood on the high south ridge of the old volcano and luxuriated in a tremendous sense of location, of knowing where we were on the high plateau lands in relation to our home, to the other mountains we've hiked, and to the ribcage of the continent itself. It was disappointing not to make the top that day, but being high and unobstructed enough to gain a greater sense of where we were in the land was still satisfying. The turnoffs at the top of mountain passes give us the same chance to mark our place, and even hardcore motor home drivers stop their unwieldy behemoths, get out to stretch, and take in the view. They point out landmarks to the family, locating themselves in the land momentarily before remounting the automotive disconnect. Though those scenic stops with their labels are also another form of landscape consumption, an invitation to a view unavoidably dictated by the highway engineers, at least they're outside the confining window of the vehicle.

The next chance to see snow will be the 12,663-foot summit of Humphrey's Peak. It's 9:11 and a train goes by as I enter the Grants city limits at an elevation of 6,470 feet. Exit #85, 16′9″. There's not much to Grants, a town of maybe 12,000 stretched out north of the freeway along a main street where only the fast-food franchises aren't boarded up. In 1950 uranium was discovered in the area, and Grants went boom and bust a couple of times over the next two decades. Despite the fact that the area outside town once produced about half the entire supply of uranium oxide in America, my guess is Grants will have to wait for an overflow of retirees from Albuquerque and Phoenix to fuel its next expansion, unless there's an unexpected demand for new nuclear power plants.

By 9:30 I'm well past Grants in a pack of three semis, and we're barreling along at 85. I'm craning my head around trying to collect as many labels as I can. I start with the moving vans—Mayflower, Bekin's, North American, Allied, United, Atlas—and then the trucks themselves—Freightliner, Peterbilt, Kenworth, International, White GMC, Mack. I'm beginning to feel as if I'm logging wildlife in a game refuge. I pass trucks carrying spools of cable, colonial furniture, and caskets—two trucks carrying caskets, in fact, one after the other, as if this were the Freeway Styx. Trucks in the opposing lanes are loaded with hay, Levi brand jeans, five red diesel engines, mail, oil, propane, dirt, and bundles of unidentified and spooky-looking gray barrels lashed tightly together. Then there are the trucks carrying other vehicles: the auto transports, of course, but there's one ferrying a bus, another with two Humvee's in camouflage drag, one of those squat airport fuel tankers being carried piggyback, and then four truck rigs—just the cabs—hiked one atop the other like elephants in a circus. I start picking out the names of the trucking companies, and get no further than Emory, Yellow, Arrow, Covenant, Digby, and Roadway before I'm completely thrown off track by a swarm of letters. Most of the trucks don't bear names at all, but triads of initials. MNX, CDI, CSW, IWX. TLC, BLM, PST, and CSC. RTC, KTL, TSL, STS. PFC, CFI, JCT, and ABF. RPS, TSL, TWT, AJF. Then there are the two- and four-letter mutants—SLLC, CRST, KLLM, RS, GT, and OTRX.

I quit before I run off the road, rest my eyes, fiddle with the radio to eke out the last of NPR's Sunday morning news from Albuquerque. They're discussing the transportation bill, and how the price of oil, adjusted for inflation, is at its lowest level in our country since World War II. Not only are there no gas lines, but we're actually exporting oil, and the Republican-run Congress is eyeing deep pools of crude underneath the Arctic Wildlife Preserve. I don't even bother to think what's wrong with this picture, but harbor the strong suspicion our children may not have the chance to go roaming about the countryside in vehicles powered by fossil fuels as I am this morning.

I cross the Continental Divide at a gentle rise, elevation of 7,275 feet, about twenty-five miles east of Gallup. A tanker truck passes me, red diamonds on its side declaring "Dangerous/Corrosive" about three feet from my nose at 80 mph. Exit #47, 16′9″. Another truck barrels past, chasing the tanker, this one bearing what looks to be a rocket nose cone poking out from underneath a tarp. "Place engine this end" is declared at the front of the trailer bed. The trucks with their threatening cargo are more immediately meaningful to me than crossing the Divide, which is just another road sign. I can't assign physical memory to hiking the Divide this far south, don't know what its temperature should be in December, or what the watershed patterns are.

At 9:52 a train passes, eastbound, and at 9:58 another, both with four engines each, accelerating hard out of Gallup to get over the Divide. At 10 A.M. and 198 miles I pass my first pedestrian. He's not hitching, just walking along with a dirty orange backpack, dressed mostly in gray with a red plaid shirt wrapped like a skirt around his waist.

THREE

Most people I know profess an intense dislike of Gallup. It's a rough town surrounded by the Navajo and Zuni reservations, oil refineries, railroad yards, and all the charming brand-name amenities of the vernacular interstate—Denny's, McDonald's, Super 8, Pizza Hut, and Best Western. The original highway through this part of the country, and one which the interstate more or less parallels, is the legendary Route 66, which is also the main street of Gallup. Unlike the interstate, that was a road synonymous with narrative, the two-lane highway traversing America and our national imagination. Now it's lined on both sides with economy motels catering to tourists seeking authentic "Indian Territory" and jewelry bargains among the streetside tables of silver and turquoise. The guidebooks warn that the alcohol-related death rate here is five times higher than the national average, and that 29,000 drunks are picked up off the streets by the Gallup police every year. Pretty amazing for a place that lists its population as only 20,000.

I wouldn't know, having just driven through or at most stopped for gas and a burger. But the physical situation of the town is one of my favorite parts of the drive. Tall cliffs of red sandstone frame the eastern approach to Gallup and a dramatic band of tan Jurassic sandstone the western entrance. The miles of steep rock as I come into town are juxtaposed with the cooling towers of power plants and complicated cracking retorts of the refineries. It's like driving into a postapocalyptic science fiction set on a back lot, and the windshield frames reality like a drive-in movie. That's appropriate, given the number of westerns filmed nearby—*Texas Rangers, The Hallelujah Trail, The Streets of Laredo.* . . . Driving a car not only cuts you off from literal contact with the world outside the window, but zips you up in a locking envelope of speed. We whiz through it all, tempted to conflate points along the way with narrative— from one overpass to the next, from Laredo, Texas, to Laredo, Hollywood. Hence my expectation this morning that dinosaurs, which lived during the time the sandstone was being formed, will come stomping through the elaborate and delicate architecture of the refineries, tails thrashing in a frenzy of demolition. No such luck. Not even Indians and cowboys on horseback.

On the outskirts of town is Indian Plaza, one of the dozens of curio shops along the interstate dressed up as trading posts. They've all taken to erecting plywood teepees around the property so you can't mistake their identity— oversized and brightly painted imitation structures which, if you could cut an entrance into them, might actually make camping spots with a strange sort of fascination. At 10:04 I spot another train going east, a line of slow black dashes proceeding through town—empty coal cars from a power plant in Arizona. It's 40 degrees, clear, and the road crews are out covering as much mileage as they can, even on a Sunday. The good weather won't last forever, and once the temperature drops too far, they can't lay asphalt. The speed limit signs are covered over, draped with white cloth as if bandaged.

At 10:20, train going west; 10:22, an Amtrak proceeding east passes a freight going the other way. I cross the border into Arizona and coast into the Painted Rock Rest Area. When I get out of the car it's warm enough to pull off my sweater, and I stroll around in a t-shirt and shorts, admiring the artworks scattered on the sandstone cliffs above me. There are life-size elk and deer, a black bear, eagle, and coyote—it's more trading post kitsch, and so poignant an emblem of what the interstate is patently not about that it should be preserved as a folk art monument to irony. It's not exactly the kind of art I had in mind when originally thinking about land and landscape—still, it's related. These hokey totems are also part of how we abstract land into a picture, this one a cliché hung over our heads from a variety of media, including the novels of James Fenimore Cooper, western movies by John Ford, and the *Lone Ranger* television series.

Back on the road, my AAA map flipped over to the new state, I'm able to pace the next train I find, a westbound freight. It's a small one, only forty-two cars with two engines, versus most of the earlier ones about twice its length.

It's clipping along at 60 mph, another assemblage of goods in circulation. I think briefly about actually trying to count both the number of train cars and trucks today, then figuring the average weight of each to derive the total tonnage encountered on the drive—but it's just too much. Somewhere in Washington, D.C., someone keeps track of such things, but I suspect just a total count of the trains, plus knowing that I'm always within sight of at least a dozen semis, is a sufficient indicator of magnitude.

At mile 237 on the odometer I pass Indian City—over two hundred brands of cigarettes, boasts one sign; another one offers "reservation prices" and 70 percent off all Indian jewelry at "Chee's Indian Store and Rock Shop." I don't think it was always called that, and I wonder what Tony Hillerman thinks of a character's name from his mystery novels being used to pull in the tourists. Four miles down the road we—the trucks and I—pass Fort Courage, touted beforehand with no fewer than twelve billboards painted in a lurid combination of yellow, red, and white. Much is promised, but basically it's just more teepees surrounding a Chevron station, a Pancake House, and another curio shop. To the right is the Rio Puerco, which means "Dirty River." In 1979 one of the upstream uranium mine holding-pond levees broke, sending 95 million gallons of radioactive water and 1,100 tons of hot mud past Gallup. The contamination was reportedly severe enough that a woman wading the flood to rescue her dog later watched the skin slough off her legs before she died. This morning the river is burnished like a silver bracelet in winter air. I pass my second pedestrian of the day, a gray-bearded hitchhiker wearing jeans and a blue windbreaker, right thumb out, looking relaxed about it all. It's 11 A.M. and I overtake another train going west.

FOUR

At mile 273 the view I've been anticipating all morning starts to open up before me to the south and west. The freeway has been steadily rising since Gallup, and now I can peer over open desert for sixty miles across the Tonto Basin and clear down to the hills atop the Mogollon Rim. The 2,000-foot-high escarpment marks the southern boundary of the Colorado Plateau and borders both the east central part of the state and the Ft. Apache Indian Reservation. It's an exhilarating clear white space on the map and out the window with no intervening green between the road and the 200-mile-long rim. To the west is a thin grouping of cirrus, roughly above the San Francisco Peaks, still over 125 miles in front of me, and the view is so immense it's as flat as a photograph, becomes for a moment "scenery," that term from the world of theater where trains would be characters on a stage and the land a backdrop to direct our attention to the foreground.

Mile 279 and I enter the boundary of the Painted Desert and the Petrified Forest, the only National Park through which I regularly drive on an interstate. Mostly what I associate with admittance to parks are entrance stations, a 35-mph speed limit, and frequent stops until we find a campsite as close as possible to the trailhead we're after. While Beth and I have detoured through the park on its twenty-eight-mile scenic loop, that's all it's been, a detour. We've not come here yet to camp and hike, though it's high on the list. Ranger statistics for Painted Desert claim that only one in every thousand tourists strays more than a few feet from his vehicles here, a number in keeping with a park bisected by an interstate, and much in our favor for when we eventually camp here. But for now I actually envy the RVs parked out on the viewpoints. Fifteen or twenty of them are clustered on a promontory oddly visible from the freeway, peering into a scenic wonder mostly invisible from the Honda. The Chinle Formation—the soft rocks stained red and orange by iron and manganese that have eroded into the scenic badlands—is capped by a harder lava flow. The dark volcanic surface not only protects the softer rocks below, but blocks most of the view from the freeway. So I'm just a spectator watching the tourists, a voyeurism oddly appropriate as I drive through the park as fast as I'm allowed.

Mile 292 and I pick up an Arizona state trooper in the inevitably white cruiser. I'm doing 75, not paying attention to the trucks, which have all slowed down before me. The cruiser stays with me for about a half mile behind one of the semis, then suddenly dashes across the median in pursuit of someone headed east. Second time this morning; we all speed back up to between 75 and 80, passing under Arizona exit #294, Sun Valley Road, 16′6″. At mile 298 I catch my first glimpse of Humphrey's Peak, Flagstaff still ninety-one miles west. A faint smudge hovers on the southern horizon, perhaps a brushfire, and though I could hardly use a pair of binoculars while driving, I'm unhappy I've once again forgotten them. It's a habit, forgetting the binos, something I usually depend on Beth to bring. Same with the camera, though while I like the power that magnification brings our unaided senses, I dislike intensely the mitigation of even the simplest camera. I don't like the view being framed, for one thing—which also accounts for my continual battle with the windshield, roofline, doorframe, and mirrors in a car. And using a camera seems to place reliance for memory upon a picture, instead of upon our imagination, a much richer matrix of recall than the two-dimensional snapshot.

There does remain for me, however, an ineluctable difference between my documenting land with a camera, and looking at art about the land, even abstract art deriving from a specific place. What you're left with, when the overnight film processing people return your prints or slides, is less than what you actually saw. The photograph is neither as detailed as what your eyes took in, nor as evocative of what your own memory can provide. It's an act of subtraction, unless you're an artist able to enlarge the frame of reference beyond the viewfinder. Artists deeply schooled in the meaning of land, not just its appearance, finesse image-making into acts of addition. Instead of allowing the inevitable frame to cut out parts of reality, they use it to focus us deeply within that reality, the land. As a result, we see and understand more than we would otherwise. And the best landscape paintings and photographs can evoke within us an almost unbearable longing for the land. Anyway, not

And using a camera seems to place reliance for memo

having such talent, I don't rue at all having left the camera behind—but the binos would be nice.

I'm back on cruise control and free to associate off the idea of a "Painted" Desert. The park started out as an addition to the original national monument of the Petrified Forest as proclaimed by Teddy Roosevelt in 1906, and the name *Painted Desert* carries with it some of the traditional American romanticism of the nineteenth century—a land created by that Ultimate Artist and turned, therefore, into a landscape calculated to elicit murmurs of appreciation for the sublime promise of nature. The officially designated viewpoint the RVs were perched upon is above the floor of the desert, vivid mesas and arroyos twisting away in all directions, a position that physically isolates you from the land and forces you to be no more than a viewer. You're above and therefore supposedly in moral domination of the wonders of nature, yet only a few yards away from the road that will take you to the visitor's center if it gets to be too hot, or too cold—or back onto the interstate if it gets to be too much of anything else. It's a very nineteenth-century attitude, closely related to our willingness to design an interstate that essentially ignores the shape of the terrain, and it derives in part from the four-hundred-year-old tradition of landscape painting in Europe.

As western Europeans and their descendants, our perception of land has been constantly transformed into one of landscape at least since the work of Claude Lorrain, the Frenchman born in 1600 who was one of the first European painters to bring landscape out from behind the human and mythical figures populating it. He turned the background into the foreground, into the middle ground, into all the ground, until land and his view of it was the entire subject of the paintings. The formula he applied was one in which a darkened foreground, typically foliage, composed a frame for the middle ground, a space in which the viewer could imagine himself and one which receded into the far distance, the misty infinity of imagination.

Those early landscape paintings—views of the land encompassed within a

oon a picture, instead of upon our imagination.

single look—began to influence not only how people looked at the country-side, but how they constructed it. The Reverend William Gilpin published guides to the English countryside at the end of the 1700s which instructed tourists how to obtain views of the countryside as if it were a painting, in other words in terms of "landscape." He encouraged the habit of visually organizing nature into picturesque vistas, an aesthetic based on the presumption that it was man's divinely granted privilege to do so. In the meantime, not being content merely to gaze over the land from naturally occurring vantage points, the English began to construct gardens that exemplified the picturesque, even going so far as to landscape their estates in order to duplicate the very paintings that established this aesthetic in the first place.

The history of our parks is inextricably mixed up with these practices and in particular with American painting and photography of the mid-1800s. John Wesley Powell, for instance, took the painter Thomas Moran with him on his third expedition down the Grand Canyon in 1873. Moran admitted to being profoundly influenced by English landscape painters. His 1874 painting, *Chasm of the Colorado,* a titanic landscape measuring seven by twelve feet, was hung in the U.S. Senate lobby, where it helped persuade Congress to create the national parks. It's not a long jump from there to the National Park Service engineering tourist viewpoints to duplicate Moran's by-then famous picture of the Grand Canyon, or the 1871 photographs of Yellowstone by William Henry Jackson, the last of the great frontier photographers. These photographs were, in yet another completion of this circle, instrumental evidence in convincing Congress to set aside the area as the first national park. The art framed the parks, and the views set forth in the paintings and photographs of the nineteenth century were duplicated closely by the park engineers as they selected the trails and viewpoints. It's a major miracle that they didn't attempt to landscape the parks in imitation of work by Moran, Albert Bierstadt, and other American artists. Later, the Atchison, Topeka, and Santa Fe Railroad even commissioned painters, Moran among them, to portray the lands served by its lines, in particular those of New Mexico and Arizona now adjacent to this interstate, which parallels the tracks.

It's not surprising that the layout of our national parks often herds us through the land in a way that borders suspiciously on the subtractive, as if the viewpoints were constructed in order that we encounter the land as a painting with a frame somehow hovering in our peripheral vision, or as a potential photograph already centered in the viewfinder. To be sure, anyone capable of hiking in the parks can soon get beyond these prepackaged vacation moments, but the parks are designed to be automobile-friendly. It's hard to avoid the seduction of collecting as many famous views in as short a time as possible, and never more so than in the Painted Desert.

Despite these thoughts and the vehement notes strewn around me in the car, I'm still envious of the RVs a few minutes ago with their long views down into the park!

FIVE

Mile 303. There isn't much to Holbrook, at least from the road. One among the many railroad towns along this route, it presents itself first with a silver water tower and some mobile homes. Then two microwave towers and a KOA campground; a MacDonald's, a supermarket, a baseball field, and a Holiday Inn. Off to one side the empty windows of a moderately stern International-style house stare vacantly into the distance, prompting the questions first, who would build such a house here, and then, second, let it fall into ruin. A Dairy Queen, a gas station or two, three more water tanks, tan this time, and that's it for the physical infrastructure visible in one pass through town at 70 mph. I count the choices available on the radio—one classical, six country, one classic rock and one contemporary, two Christian, and two adult soft-rock mush—thirteen stations coming from all points of the compass: Farmington, Flagstaff, Gallup, Phoenix. One of the country singers is lamenting that he's married to a waitress and doesn't even know her name. What Holbrook does offer the retirees camped out in their doublewides is Exit #283, 15′10″ and a view south over the edge of absolutely nowhere. It's flat-out magnificent, and there's a road that heads straight through it, State Highway 77, that eventually terminates in Show Low, a small town up on the road paralleling the rim. It's an alternative route to Phoenix from Santa Fe, and one I'll take sometime. Now, though, it's on to Winslow.

Mile 310 brings me to one of my favorite power plants in all of America. I'm not that fond of coal-burning power plants, especially those in the desert that put out what look to be perfectly innocent plumes of almost invisible emissions. In the aggregate, over hundreds of miles and many years, those fine particulates enfog us as surely and visibly as traffic on the San Bernardino Freeway has shrouded the remaining palm trees and orange groves of Redlands, California, in acid smog. The photographer John Pfahl has done an entire series on smoke and smokestacks in America, among them the power plants of the Southwest. His images are exquisite, verging on that romantic sublime, the color of toxic emissions as rich and soft as the sunset at an expensive resort. But his work also carries such condemnatory authority that never should anyone, anywhere, ever doubt our power to pollute. Pfahl and other artists know all too well that our interventions in the land, no matter how destructive, can appear to be beautiful, and they use that irony to great advantage in their art, playing our historical stereotypes of what we suppose to be wilderness against the reality of what we suppose to be civilization.

Likewise, the juxtaposition of a large piece of industrial architecture with the empty desert can also appear romantic. We are still very much saddled with our notion that man's erection of machinery in the wilderness is evidence of our prowess, our economic and technological ability to use the world to our advantage. Our hearts still flutter with a trace of that eighteenth-century passion, where puny men dare to challenge big mountains and vast deserts with the tools of civilization in order to "conquer" the wilderness.

This Arizona power plant to my left, with its two huge stacks and enormous pile of black coal, situated at 5,000 feet above sea level, has as its backdrop today two things—that enormous draw of land outside of Holbrook, and the growing evidence of what does, indeed, look to be a fire to the south and west, which is sobering. Just as I start righteously to dissect how we worship "the terrible sublime" in our environmental depredations, nature kicks in with a reminder that, yes, while we're doing our best to kill ourselves in more ways than one, nature still provides its own hazards. Think smoke from the power plant isn't all that bad? Then add it to the long list of other atmospheric emissions our lungs try to cope with daily, including forest- and brushfires, natural or otherwise. I can't tell how big the fire is, probably even if I had the binoculars, but the smoke is being pushed out by the prevailing westerlies high up for miles and miles. Ten miles? Twenty? A hundred? It looks like it's all the way down in the national forest lands of the rim, so who knows? I pass Exit #274, 16'7", and at 11:53 a freight going east with over a hundred cars. The plume from the power plant becomes invisible, but the forest fire smoke remains on the horizon.

SIX

I'm now catching up to or passing trains every five to fifteen minutes, and cross the Little Colorado River in Winslow around 12:20 P.M. The water is about two yards wide and looks all of six inches deep, though the size of the channel and steeply cut banks argue for torrential monsoon downpours in late summer and flashfloods strong enough to drown any vehicle that would care to be in the way. The earth color goes to deep red west of town, and I'm now close enough to Flagstaff and the San Francisco Mountains to see there's no snow there, either. Just before Two Guns with its fake teepees—which is, in turn, just before Twin Arrows with its comparable architectural adornments—I pass the turnoff to Meteor Crater. The tipoff, in case one misses the signs, isn't teepees, but a hemispherical building with a crest on top that vaguely suggests invading aliens. It's more of that science fiction we accept as appropriate for the desert, evidence of that invasion beamed into our televisions from Hollywood, which set aliens in the desert because that was the nearest available topography, the film industry previously having moved from the East Coast to the West for the sake of "westerns." We've grown up to accept the possibility, maybe even the probability, of wagon trains outside Gallup and spaceships in Winslow. And the funky building advertising Meteor Crater makes literal sense to the I-40 drivers; only out here can we actually see an entire and very, very big hole in the ground made by something that fell from outer space. It's not overgrown by Central American jungle or Siberian forest, as are other prehistoric craters, but flat-out naked and exposed in the desert for us to just drive right up and gawk into, another example of the awe-inspiring terrible-sublime we routinely expect of the West in general and the desert in particular.

There are artists who work on a scale—well, if not exactly to rival this size of things in the desert, at least to deal with it outside the frame of a photograph or a painting. The plywood teepees aren't built large simply out of a sense of playful excess—no business pays for more square inches of advertising than it has to—but because the land is itself so open and vast. If you don't match the scale of the environment, not to mention the speed of the traffic and what it does to visual acuity and our ability to read, you'll be overlooked. What the roadside advertisers know is connected directly to issues dealt with by artists working in the region. Advertising is, after all, a task-driven version of the visual arts.

Robert Smithson is credited as the first artist to work directly on the land at a large scale (though there are several other artists, not to mention a few tribes in the Americas and a host of folk artists who might find such a claim both amusing and infuriating). His *Spiral Jetty,* constructed in late 1970 on the northeastern shore of the Great Salt Lake, is the prime example, a 1,500-foot-long rock sculpture bulldozed and piled out from the shore to form a large spiral alternately flooded over and revealed, depending on the level of the lake. Several ideas impelled Smithson to make such a piece, one of which was to make art so large that it escaped the confining frame of the gallery itself, both its visual and capitalistic constraints. Another was to create a heroic sculpture on par with the paintings of Jackson Pollock, whose work was so large and energetic his canvases had to be laid out on the floor to receive and hold the paint hurled by the artist. *Spiral Jetty* is large enough to drive out on, both a practical construction technique and a necessity for sculpture in a land so open to the eye.

While it certainly achieves the latter goal, effectively tugging at our definition of romantic heroism through a size so large it can't be overlooked, Smithson didn't completely escape the gallery frame. Sculpture at this scale and placed in the land may not reside within four walls, but several such pieces are now owned by museums and other organizations, and thus exist at least partially in an institutional framework.

There have been a host of people working directly on the land since, but three notable ones have created—or are in the process of creating—large works in the three states of my Sunday drive: Walter de Maria with *Lightning Field* in western New Mexico, James Turrell at the *Roden Crater* project just west and north of my current position on I-40, and *City* by Michael Heizer in remote central eastern Nevada. *Lightning Field,* owned and operated by the Dia Center for the Arts in New York City, consists of 400 stainless steel rods averaging over 20 feet high, and posted 225 feet apart in a gridwork roughly one mile by one kilometer. It's a shimmering and fey installation inserted literally into and made part of the ground, and Dia's rules require that you stay overnight to experience it. You live temporarily on the very land with the sculpture, and are therefore a deliberate part of the piece and the process by which it cohabits the land, whether or not there's a thunderstorm present and lightning attracted. There's not really any privileged viewpoint from which to

1. Aerial view of Roden Crater from the south, c. 1980. Photograph by James Turrell.

experience the piece, though you would hope you're in the guest quarters during a storm. The word "*landscape*" migrated from the Dutch and over into English around 1600, shortly before Lorrain began painting, and was appropriated by artists to delineate a piece of art representing the land, as opposed to a seascape, portraiture, or a still life. The word also implies a fixed point of view *toward,* but never in reality *into,* the land depicted, all the tricks of perspective notwithstanding. Obviously, de Maria has seriously adjusted the meaning of the word.

Turrell's *Roden Crater* deals with one of the innumerable small cinder cones in front and to the right of me as I pass over the Babbitt Tank Wash; and at mile 370 I've come to one of the almost completely empty views on the entire trip—a stretch of relatively level road reaching west to the foot of Humphrey's Peak with no habitation in sight. The San Francisco volcanic field lies just east-northeast of the peak and contains over four hundred extinct volcanoes, an area Turrell scouted from his private plane in 1974 while flying over the western United States in search of a site for his new sculpture. From the top of Roden Crater, the geological feature, as opposed to *Roden Crater,* the artwork, you can see both Humphrey's and the Painted Desert, as well as the gorge of the Little Colorado River.

Turrell's been reshaping his cinder cone, which he bought, since 1979, leveling off its rim, drawing up plans for various tunnels and underground chambers for viewing the sky, and hiring other artists to execute topographical drawings of the project, which are published and sold in various forms to raise money for the work. It's been said that he may never finish the piece, but if he does, it promises to be worth a visit. Turrell's work since the 1960s has mostly concerned itself with light, a medium he has learned to manipulate so well that it forms apparently physical volumes when encountered in gallery installations. Simply by modifying interior spaces, thus directing and concentrating both natural and manmade light, Turrell makes empty space so palpable that you have trouble walking into it, fearful you're going to bump into a solid wall. *Roden Crater* combines his preoccupation over light, space, and color with nature. Turrell is very suspicious of how we look at nature and try to turn it into art, and is creating, instead, art as place where we are directly in contact with nature.

To do so, he's jumped out of traditional architectural space and into the curvilinear realm of the extinct volcano, using the horizon and the sky to frame our perceptions. *Roden Crater* is thus part prehistorical observatory, part postmodern sculpture, part scenic overlook.

Not only is Turrell working at the scale of the desert itself, unobtrusively modifying a visible feature of it—but he's playing a sly game with the Meteor Crater folk down the road. Instead of pointing a finger down into the crater and speculating on how big the explosion was—shivering in the presence of the sublime, as it were—he's gesturing upward. When we look at a horizon line, whether in the real world or in a piece of art, we're usually more interested in what lies on or below it, either a figure on the land, or the land itself. Turrell has us consider the upper other half of the picture, the sky, which is visually as large or larger than the land, a strategy designed to help us to consider scale, land, and landscape. Of course, it doesn't hurt that, in order to reach the piece, he's planned an approach on foot of several miles. No driving up to this attraction in your air-conditioned RV.

Heizer is up to something entirely different from de Maria and Turrell. He does sometimes push earth around with big machines, creating among other things very large holes in the desert, such as the *Double Negative* cut in 1969—70 into Mormon Mesa north of Las Vegas (owned by and in the collection, if not within the literal walls, of the Museum of Contemporary Art in Los Angeles). When I use the term *large,* I mean *Double Negative* is 1,500 feet in length and displaces 240,000 tons of earth. So his sculptures are not insignificant in terms of size, and in fact his *Effigy Tumuli* series on the banks of the Illinois River is the largest sculpture in the world. Another project to which Heizer has devoted much money, time, and energy is located on his property in a valley northeast of the Nevada Test Site. *City* was begun in 1972 with construction of *Complex One,* a remarkable work featured on the cover of "*Artforum.*" That cover took your breath away. *Complex One,* 110 by 140 by 23½ feet high, is an earthen bunker faced with earth-colored concrete and defined by a series of massive beams thrusting into space. The sculpture was monumentally architectonic, simultaneously archaic yet utterly contemporary. It was huge and threatening and made it look as if a new civilization had been discovered on earth. The cover photo didn't indicate an imitation of a theoretical "Sublime," but a piece of it made manifest in the Nevada desert that we could imagine touching.

I walked the thirty feet out onto the tip of the forward projecting beam last year and stood looking west while Beth crossed her fingers against a stray breeze. Before me spread out the rest of *City* constructed to date, a giant field excavated about twenty feet below grade. Carved into a series of large bays, some holding giant concrete stele like ancient Mesoamerican writing tablets, *City* is both geometric and organic, foreign and familiar. When standing in the middle of the excavation, as we're meant to do, nothing but the horizon of the sculpture itself and the sky are visible. It's comprehensible to the eye in one full turn of the body, yet utterly strange. There's nothing else like it that I know of in the history of either sculpture or landscape, natural or built. It absolutely bends us into consideration of several things simultaneously: How land looks, and how we transform it into landscape by physically altering both the land and our view of it; how we have done this throughout history and prehistory; what we reckon to be size and how that relates to scale in landscape; the relationship between utility, land, and value—numerous enough considerations, in fact, that critics from around the world are constantly writing about it.

The point is that it's helpful to avoid the "viewpoint" we take for granted, that singular stance we assume before a piece of art or behind the windshield of a car. All three of these works require time and effort to reach, and time spent actually inside the pieces themselves. They are part of the land, not separated from it as discrete objects. The idea is for us to be inside the works and thus engaged with the land. We not only place ourselves literally in the landscape (the art about the land, a mark on the land, a "landmark" made by the artist), but we're shifting our mental placement of land in the hierarchy of our values. That's to say, by experiencing these sculptures we are led to value the land more highly, approaching not simply the appearance of it, but also the meaning. We're no longer voyeurs of the theoretical Sublime with a capital "S," as we are at the rim of a landscape painting by Bierstadt, or at the edge of Meteor Crater, or driving by those turnouts in the Painted Desert—but, rather, we are in it, participants in the creation of a personal sublime with a lowercase "s."

Walking around inside these artworks is, once again, to place ourselves in a direct relationship with the land, and as surely as I'm attempting to quantify this trip by counting everything from overpasses to pedestrians, so walking becomes a "pacing off," a measuring. Walking makes manifest the story of our lives through an activity that is both literal and metaphorical; it takes us off of the privileged viewpoint, whether that's in front of a painting or staring over a guardrail at the Painted Desert. I say let's have de Maria, Turrell, and Heizer design the national parks.

SEVEN

Mile 375, not quite quarter of one in the afternoon, and I pass over Padre Canyon, unable to see anything because of those concrete modular roadside barriers. I hate those things, the person who invented them, and the officious bureaucrat who decided every federal road passing over anything interesting should include them. No wonder pickup trucks are the fastest selling vehicles in America—they're about the only way you can see over the damn things. So much for the sublime on the interstates. I'm consoled by the

"Watch for Elk" sign outside Flagstaff as we enter the pine trees, and take an early exit into town for gas at mile 397.

The air is cool, the sun hot as I stretch. It's a luxury to be able to pay the cashier after filling up, in contrast with the insistent paranoia of gas stations in urban New Mexico, where you're obliged to pay the attendant beforehand. I feel as if I'm back in college days, on the road and pumping miles: 7.73 gallons for 397 miles. At 51 miles to the gallon, though, my fuel efficiency is almost twice that of the cars I owned in the sixties. I get back on the freeway as quickly as I can, anxious not to lose my place among the trucks I've been passing for the last few hours. I slip in among eight semis alongside a white Camaro and a pickup truck. The yellow Dodge Ram is piloted by a matching blonde with bare forearms, intent on keeping her high-centered ton-and-a-half mass in the right-hand lane despite the buffeting from the trailer rigs.

Just west of the last Flagstaff exit all eleven of our vehicles come up to and seemingly float over a crest in the road, the Arizona Divide. At an elevation of 7,355 above sea level, it's eighty feet higher than the unremarkable Continental Divide I drove over in New Mexico. And while Flagstaff's not the literal halfway point on this trip, which I passed somewhere between Holbrook and Winslow, it's definitely my psychic divide. This crest in Arizona marks our passage from the Atlantic drainage of the Colorado Plateau to the Pacific drainage of the Colorado River Basin, and into a transition zone that's half northern Sonoran and half Mojave Desert. It's at first a wetter terrain but, as we slowly descend, will grow increasingly dryer and hotter, more and more like the Mojave Desert as we approach Kingman. Physiographically, this trip takes me west across the lower part of the Colorado Plateau, turning aside before I can get south enough to touch the Chihuahuan Desert, then proceeds through the Painted and a bit of the Sonoran, then across a corner of the Mojave to Las Vegas, where I'm almost within sight of the highest and coldest of North America's five deserts, the Great Basin. It's a grand traverse of our drylands done as a Sunday drive, and I recommend it most especially to residents of the New England and the mid-Atlantic states. All of New England, for instance, would fit into any one of the three states I'm in today, with room left over for the Hawaiian Islands and the Atomic Test Site.

Passing over the Arizona Divide we also pick up the first sign for Los Angeles, 487 miles to the west, mecca for all lovers of the automobile culture and the terminus of the Old Spanish Trail, the original trade route from Santa Fe that passed through the oasis of Las Vegas. By the time I-40 terminates at Barstow in the middle of the Mojave, the air quality reminds you that less than an hour ahead is an atmospheric graveyard called the San Bernardino Valley, where begins a megalopolis of traffic so slow you feel like a fixture on the freeway and not a passenger over it. As if to echo that sentiment while still deep in the highlands of Arizona, though, there's another forest fire, this one in a valley to the immediate left, its orange line a half-mile long. We pass through a cloud of wet-smelling smoke that tastes remarkably like the winter evening air in San Bernardino, a mixture of fog and smog so acidic it eats the paint off cars.

I'm not sure if it's the mileage sign for L.A., that magnet of commerce for many of the trucks on this road, or simply the beginning of the long descent toward the California border, but we're all doing 80 when we pass an Arizona

Drive long enough on the interstate in a single day and you'll not on

cop with a white Jeep Cherokee who's pulled over a truck on the other side of the freeway. We slow down to 70, reminded by the Jeep that this is snow country in winter, despite our wearing shirtsleeves in this December. A Cadillac with Texas plates passes me, well over the centerline, reaffirming my dislike not only of Cadillacs, but of Texans driving them, a combination that apparently induces total obliviousness to anyone else on the pavement, whether they're in downtown Santa Fe or out here on the relatively open road. Then a U-Haul rental truck with a trailer from New Jersey passes me going 75, twenty miles over the posted limit for such vehicles. It, too, is over the white line, and I remind myself that Texans aren't any worse than the rest of us. But I reserve my judgment on Cadillacs.

Mile 420, 1:28 P.M., Blue Springs Road, 16′6″. Mile 442, and signs warn of a 6 percent downhill grade; the brake check area beforehand is full of trucks, drivers circling their rigs on foot, thumping tires with metal bars. It's warm enough in the low sun of early afternoon to crack a window. Mile 486, a state trooper has pulled over a white sedan. Except for the blue stripe on the cruiser the two cars are almost identical, white being the preferred choice for vehicles in hot climates. Just try to buy a blue automobile in Albuquerque, Phoenix, or Las Vegas, and you'll immediately discover how car dealers reinforce the local palette of automotive culture. By mile 489 the trucks outnumber cars 2:1. I'm doing 75 and a Navajo tribal cop passes me going 80, rousing me from an hour which has disappeared into the stupefying mental hiss of interstate self-absorption. If running produces an endorphin high after about forty-five minutes, where you gently disassociate from your surroundings and the state of your knees in a mild euphoria, then freeway cruising breeds a state of numbness akin to anesthesia. Drive long enough on the interstate in a single day and you'll not only forget you have knees, but lose touch with

orget you have knees, but lose touch with what planet you're on.

what planet you're on. I'm still counting overpasses, keeping tabs on the trip odometer and clock, watching for state troopers and road kill, but it's all been done on autopilot, as if I were taking a nap in the middle of the trip.

I come out of my trance in time to read a sign announcing land in Bridge Canyon for sale at $3,495 an acre. It's pleasant enough country, sparse forest mixed with grasslands about eighty miles west of Flagstaff, still barely within range of the public radio station there—but what on earth is the reason for a subdivision of ranchettes here? There's a red and white radio tower, a highway maintenance station with three or four metal buildings, and no services, gas, food, or lodging that I can see. I can only take it for a sign of how we're infilling real estate along the road. When I was a kid, I'd accompany my parents on drives at night across the desert. No one had air conditioning in their cars in the fifties; and anyway, who would be foolish enough to drive the desert in daylight? There were long stretches where the only other visible lights were stars, and every now and then another pair of headlights. Occasionally, and much to the discomfort of my mother, my father would shut off our lights on an empty straightaway, and we'd hum along quietly in the dark with nothing but that dim starlight reflecting off the desert floor. But in the last five years, I can't recall a single stretch of interstate where you're entirely away from lights by the side of the road, not to mention constant traffic.

Mile 496, the Jolly Rd. overpass, 16'6"; it's 2:30, 440 miles to L.A. and about 50 to Kingman, yet another town born of the railroad. Fifteen minutes later and I'm passing by the Willow Ranch exit (16' even, a rarity). There's a road-cut featuring beautifully folded layers of rock, stacked both vertically and horizontally in a frenzy of geological excess, and then we're in the middle of the ranch, literally, fields of a young winter crop that look to be alfalfa spread out not only to the right, but to the left in acreage in between the east- and westbound lanes. It's a brief pastoral before we drop into sage and mesquite, then the rocky canyon that both Willow Creek and the freeway follow down into the desert.

Coming out of the canyon at 4,000 feet the view opens up to the compact and rocky peaks typical of Arizona's arid lowlands. The Sonoran Desert, which genuinely begins south of here, is the wettest of the five deserts, lush compared to the Chihuahuan and Mojave, but still a shockingly austere region compared to the forested uplands out of which we've all just descended. The only radio station I'm now picking up is drilling through a set of Iron Butterfly and Led Zeppelin, music that I fear will outlast everything from Mozart to the Talking Heads and become the tribal punk of the next millennium. Fitting ditties for Kingman, that bastion of militant antigovernment survivalists and the FBI personnel who maintain surveillance on their tract homes and apartments, which spread out into the surrounding basin like Styrofoam litter. At mile 542, still east but now in view of Kingman itself, I pass the first sign for Las Vegas: 103 miles.

Two semis loaded with hot-tub minispas are airbraking and downshifting toward an exit with a MacDonald's, and I trail along. We take a complicated loop down to a surface boulevard, and I squeeze around the trucks to the MacParking Lot. I get out and take my final stretch of the drive, purchase a cup of coffee to go, and once back in the car retrieve a piece of leftover birthday cake Beth has sent with me. There's a skinny older guy dressed in a brown imitation leather jacket going through the two waste receptacles out front for aluminum cans; his bag is almost full, and I wonder what it's like to "retire" in the sunny community of Kingman, mining garbage to earn enough change to eat. Maybe the survivalists are right to be stocking up on canned food. I'm back on the freeway in ten minutes, glad to be getting through town as fast as I can.

EIGHT

Before exiting Kingman through a low pass to the west, the freeway takes me past a relatively new residential development built up along a golf course. I've driven by before when it's absolutely green and verdant—even in the middle of the hottest months—but right now there's a guy on a tractor mower who's chewing as much dust as brown grass. Apart from wondering who would want to move to Kingman in order to live on a golf course in the middle of one of the driest places in America—which is to question, as well, who'd want to live so shamelessly exposed to the wonderment of passersby on the freeway—apart from basic bafflement, I can't summon up much outrage this late in the drive. Once over that small pass the golf course is out of sight and I exit onto State Highway 93. For the first time since leaving the Rio Grande Valley, I turn parallel to the structure of the land, going north and parallel with the mountains instead of cutting across them. Immediately it's hotter and dryer, and although I'm still in Arizona, it begins to feel more like the accordion valleys and mountains of Nevada than the classic sandstone territory of the Southwest.

This road is a particularly unforgiving one. The sun is down to the last quarter of the sky, and the peaks are beginning to take on that warm glow so eagerly sought after by photographers. It's a handsome country with which I'm familiar, having lived in the basin-and-range province for thirty-three years; but, more often than you'd care to see, there are those white crosses on the road marking a fatality. Highway 93 has been only two lanes from Kingman to Las Vegas for most of its life, in the last few years grudgingly widened piece by piece into a four-lane road with a median. Las Vegas cultivates the late-night culture and offers free drinks at the casinos. Not a particularly safe combination, night driving on a fast and narrow highway when you're tired and maybe drunk. Head-on collisions and rollovers are endemic, though the recent widening helps separate things out.

Only a few trucks are on the road, most of the haulage having continued west to L.A., and there are no more overpasses to count until the Las Vegas Valley. To the east there's a range of mountains rising to over 7,000 feet, and a containment wall for the huge cyanide leaching ponds of a gold mining company, an earthen bulwark reminiscent of Heizer's *Complex One.* A dirt road leads off to the right for the remnants of Chloride, a mining town from the last century; to the west there's a dust devil and an even higher set of peaks. Giant cholla cacti crook their skinny arms at all angles, and a cop writes up the driver of a small pickup truck. Sand-blasted gas stations, bars, mobile homes, and the inevitable junkyards of rust that punctuate the desert highways of the 1990s are all I pass from 3:30 P.M. until 4:22. At mile 607 I pass the exit for Temple Bar, part of the Lake Mead National Recreation Area above Hoover

Dam. There's a glimpse of the lake, then I'm crossing under a set of huge powerlines from the dam, rising up into a gap in the hills bordering the recreation area, and into a moment worth the entire drive.

It's a classic desert sandbag. The mountains and valleys of the basin and range are so large and uniform in size and rhythm that you're taken completely aback when you breach the rim of the Colorado River. Edge after edge of folded, stacked, and immensely complex mountain ridges rear up before you. At 65 mph and negotiating the first curves in an hour, it seems as if you've driven onto the moon. The 1,500-foot cliffs of the Black Canyon appear sterile, every edge razor-sharp, and miles below you can see a bend in the river itself before it winds out of sight. The land has gone from merely austere to genuinely desolate and intimidating, the most abrupt shift in the view all day.

From here Highway 93 bores through a succession of road cuts and desiccated gullies until it reaches an overlook above the dam. Although that first view of the river remains my favorite moment of the trip, this isn't half bad, and I always pull off for a look. The entire area is a scenic anomaly of the severest order, where what would otherwise be a heart-stopping natural gorge collides with the Industrial Age and becomes a bathtub. The Colorado River should wind darkly through the narrows of Black Canyon here; instead, the nine-trillion-gallon Lake Mead forms an 822-mile-long placid shoreline complete with a white ring circling the canyon walls at the highwater mark. The dam, hundreds of miles of mega-voltage power lines, and assorted paraphernalia of commercial energy carrying four billion kilowatt-hours of electricity each year are held literally and figuratively in high tension against the ground and over the water. I can't help but hear in my head that warning about the danger of balancing electrical appliances on the rim of the tub.

The surrounding rock walls are bare of vegetation with the road carved out in switchbacks on both sides of the canyon, and I start the 15-mph crawl in light traffic down to the dam, amazed as always that there are at least a dozen semis pulled off at the various small overlooks. Their drivers, who otherwise break every legal highway convention ever invented in order to make time, are perched on retaining walls, legs dangling, smoking cigarettes, and gazing around. I imagine what it must be like to fold your truck and trailer around the tight curves, sinking down into and then laboriously shifting up out of the canyon.

Clocks reside high on the towers at each end of the dam, first the Arizona one at 4:36 P.M. and then the Nevada one at 3:46 P.M. I set back the Honda's clock as I climb up into Nevada, enjoying the distortion of scale in this landscape. The power lines and their towers, the way they're cantilevered over the abyss and anchored with thick cables, are unmistakably massive, but the dam itself is too large to comprehend unless you walk across it, enumerate it with footsteps the way you do very large mountain peaks, which so overshadow their surroundings that they actually look small. The scenery here makes you feel as if you're a kid playing in the dirt again, diverting water from the garden hose and building bridges with twigs. That's the nearest and most readily available visual analog for the difference in size between ourselves as individuals and the collective construction of Hoover Dam. On the one hand is the miniature and on the other the huge, both very much out of sync with our otherwise pragmatic scale of the world through which we drive or walk.

As always, I derive an element of pleasure out of Hoover Dam that's related to one I get from that gold mine's containment wall back down the road, and Michael Heizer's *City,* and even the power plant outside Holbrook. Not so much about size as about scale in the natural world, the artificial structures each relate to and derive power from the land in unique ways, but always within the upper reaches of what is technically feasible for us to build. Much of the emotional power generated by Heizer's sculptures stems from the genuinely heroic effort it takes to displace so much earth, an effort we can't help but admire also at the mines and the dam, or in the elaborate labyrinth of the coal-fired power plant. The Industrial Sublime, that aesthetic label we affix

2. Mark Klett, *Holding Lake Mead: Hoover Dam, 7/85.*

to large manmade structures placed in juxtaposition to the natural world, still taps into the root of pretechnological wonderment. Even as we decry the massive environmental disturbance and the conversion of resource into consumption, we marvel at the constructions and unconsciously flex our muscles.

A few minutes later I pass a startlingly out-of-place hotel-casino, the first outpost for Las Vegas, just past which there's a Nevada Highway Patrol car parked to observe the road coming in from the lake on the left. It's Sunday night and the trolling is good—drunken boaters on their way back into town are fair game and plentiful. Around a curve or two is Boulder City, elevation 2,507 feet, most of which I bypass on the truck route. My last empty view of the day is of the valley stretching south toward the town of Searchlight, the sky cloudy but sunlight breaking through to pick out the dust plume from a vehicle on a dirt road twenty miles downhill. The driver out there has wheels to the earth and is marking off distance with dust, a view which realigns my sense of scale still reeling from Hoover Dam. The land is large, the cars remain small, the distances to be covered available to great speed. Then it's over Railroad Pass, where 95 merges into the newly extended Interstate 515, and the entire valley below fills with white stucco subdivisions arrayed around the neon Strip.

It's sunset and the lights are coming on. Las Vegas is a giant garden folly from an earlier century, some architectural phantasmagoria coming to life in the early evening. I pass under a pair of new curvilinear overpasses, no height given, the clearance assumed by everyone to be sufficient in a state of legalized gambling.

NINE

Seventy-three overpasses, twenty trains, eight law enforcement vehicles, two pedestrians, and four road kill; 632 miles in just under ten hours, about an hour less than the AAA map suggests—and that's all I can count. Pitiful. I can't tell you how many rivers, streams, and washes I crossed, the number of trucks, cars, or even towns passed without referring to a map. Compared to desert tribespeople, I'm totally number impaired, unable to remember the number of strides between waterholes. I've made notes and slash marks, have maps and guidebooks for reference, and I still won't get it all exactly correct.

As I coast down the off ramp, I also remind myself that this is the point: interstates are designed to isolate you from the surroundings. For the most part, freeways don't respect land. The engineers are compelled to consider it as terrain to be negotiated in the most time- and energy-efficient manner. In essence, they deliberately diminish the land into a straight and level landscape, transforming land into backdrop scenery, in order to transport people and their goods without loss of speed or the potential impediment of thought. Interstates are meant to be survived at speed, and that means a road with as few visual and mental temptations as possible. The road itself, then, mitigates against counting. Its calculated bland façade and the speed it insists upon are a complex economic equation that allows no point of view but that of progress along the road itself. The only anomalous events we witness are interruptions of flow, whether those are large scale, as in road construction, or at the individual level, as in someone being ticketed by the side of the road. And the flow, that mind-numbing arterial rush, works only at speed; once we're delayed on the interstate beyond a few minutes its entire meaning is threatened, and we become aggressive in the face of some interminable delay between us and our destiny.

It's not simply destination to which we feel entitled by the interstates, but we consider it our continuing and irresistible purpose to be as mobile as we please in the fulfillment of our destiny as masters of the land. Instead of knowing the land, however, we have substituted speed, estimated time of arrival, and fuel consumption for genuine narrative. We're insulated from temperature, local fragrance, and sound, our windows up against the exhaust from other cars and the backwash from semis. It's not that driving has to be this way, or that walking is the only virtuous mode of transportation. When interrupted on two-lane highways, for instance, which are less commanding toward and more intimate with the terrain, we often accept interruptions as an excuse to admire the location. Speed simply isn't the purpose of those roads, though sometimes it's part of their joy.

I exit from freeway to street, a dizzying and disorienting slowdown to 35 mph, stop signs, pedestrians, and driveways, and realize I'm making a mental transition from the vacuum of the interstate to neighborhood and back to narrative. It's like stepping off a long and fast moving walkway, when, no matter how carefully you've calculated your exit, the first step wobbles uncertainly. I roll down the window and turn left, downhill and deeper into the suburb, a tired, stiff, and hungry driver. I count the number of blocks to the street where my friends live and I'll stay the night. I count the houses to their driveway, in this case not out of any higher desire to prove a point, but just exercising a simple navigational skill. I've kept my place in the stream of travel and have a story to tell over dinner.

Los Angeles to Las Vegas

Counting Backwards

THREE

October 31, 1996

We hear the helicopters in Los Angeles before we see them, and it's not until I set the odometer at zero and turn left onto 6th Street that I can spot the one hovering a couple of hundred feet up and about three blocks east. Helicopters in our neighborhood come in two varieties, the cops and the newspeople chasing the cops, and from this distance I can't tell which it is. Less than three minutes into my drive I'm diverted away from a two-car crash that's accordioned one car down to the size of a steamer trunk, and bent the other into a horseshoe around the driver's door. Two full-length hook-and-ladders, three ambulances, and more police cars than I can count block the intersection. The helicopter is Channel 7 Action News, and I detour underneath it over to 4th, wondering about injuries—and the fact that Beth often drives this way to work.

I jog back over to 6th and at 11:38, eight minutes and 2.5 miles from home, I'm in front of where my great-grandmother lived at 628 Irving Street. The tan-painted brick house has deep Prairie-style eaves, vaguely Tudorish beams dressing the front, and a mixed-breed front porch. White curtains hang in the downstairs windows, though I catch a glimpse of dark wainscotting inside. Despite the architectural pastiche, it retains an air of midwestern sobriety among its more fanciful Norman and Georgian neighbors. It's also a solid piece of bilateral symmetry so carefully proportioned that it's not until I'm leaving that I realize it's three stories high, not two. As I drive away, watched by a woman from upstairs next door, I'm still thinking the house doesn't look all that large. Then I remember the inherited linen tablecloth we have at home, the one we can't use because Mrs. Lyman's dining room table seated sixteen people. Tables that long don't fit in small rooms; rooms that large don't fit into small houses.

I haven't spent more than a minute in front of the property, knowing I'll swing by to pay homage on those occasional days I drop Beth at the metro station a few blocks away. I turn right onto Wilshire and join the late-morning-bus crawl, the suits-in-black-German-machines-on-their-cell-phone crawl. I should count the stoplights but forget. Twenty minutes later I'm on Palm Drive heading north, detouring as necessary to cross from L.A. to Beverly Hills, a mysterious boundary where the direction, numbering, and other logical paraphernalia of civic engineering are suspended in order to confuse aliens like me. At 12:09 P.M. and 10.1 miles on the odometer I'm in front of my maternal grandfather's house, 622 Palm. Thirty minutes to cover 7.6 miles, which in midday traffic isn't all that bad.

This is a house of which I have no recollection whatsoever, William Henry Lyman, Jr. having died of yellow fever in Kobe, Japan, on the last day of January 1936, thirteen years before my birth. His first wife, my grandmother Olive de Ressel, had also died by the time I was born, and the second wife who shared this house with Grandfather Lyman has been expunged from family records by my mother, who banished her as a wicked stepmother into some obscure closet of her memory. The house is a white two-story stucco with a red-tile roof and brick trim. While its roofline carries deep eaves in common with Great-grandmother's house, it's definitely more refined and exotic, and even more eclectic in style. Two immense magnolia trees shade the front and a late model Jag is parked in back, the property framed behind a lawn too perfect to be cared for personally by its owners. There's no one in sight, but I feel more scrutinized than on Irving Street—Beverly Hills does that to you—so I leave after about fifteen seconds. Maybe I'll bring Beth back, just so she can see it, but the only reason I even know this house exists within the family geography is because of Grandfather's will stashed underneath my desk in the safebox.

And now the slowest part of the trip, the second leg of the triangle down Sunset Boulevard through Hollywood, the route I imagine my parents might have taken from one grandparent's house to the other. Maybe the Strip was more glamorous in the 1930s, not as dense and polyglot. Now the tattoo parlors boast "Quality piercing since 1975," and the Russian émigrés, runaway teenagers, hookers, and tourists have only really collided in the nineties'. The 3.3 miles to Mclaren Fox's old house at 704 Las Palmas Ave. takes seventeen minutes, the clock at 12:26 when I pull up at the corner of Melrose and Las Palmas. The neighborhood here is residential bordering on commercial, and the cars parked in the cracked driveway of the single-story Spanish-style bungalow are clean but tattered compacts. I remember a lawn, but now there's a screen of low bushes on the corner to cut down the noise and glare, and cacti underneath the barred windows in front, a double line of defense. Grandmother Fox was a short, slight Parisian, Mac a hulking Scotsman who was head of the local Associated Press bureau. Neither of them would have liked the wrought-iron bars twisted in front of the living room view. I don't spend much time here, either, and arrive back home at 12:36 having driven seventeen miles intersecting three generations of family.

We moved to Los Angeles from Santa Fe a month ago, Beth flying in ahead to start a new job, me following in the car with art, manuscripts, and computer equipment. I not only retraced my route from the previous trip to Las Vegas, but continued to its logical conclusion, Wilshire Boulevard, which a few miles west from our townhouse terminates abruptly on the bluffs in Santa Monica above the Pacific Ocean. This is where 4,500 years or more of one phase in the expansion of the human race ends, westward from Babel to Babylon, and I'm not exactly sure how to place my memories here, or how to remember this place. In the psychic middle of my personal journey here, if not the march of civilization, is Las Vegas, which I take to be a pivot point in Western landscape and culture.

Next month on the twenty-first we'll be driving back to Santa Fe, passing through Las Vegas on the way, and this time Beth will drive. She's looking forward to taking our new Honda on its first road trip (the old blue one having gone shamefully, irreparably over the mileage limits of its lease, much to the woe of our checkbook). I won't have to risk taking out several interstate trucking companies in a massive pileup while looking around, writing, counting, and changing radio stations at the same time as, incidentally, driving. This trip will be the second stage in what's turning out to be a triangulation of Las Vegas, part of my investigation into landscape, driving, and memory.

54

I finally figured this out last week as I was unpacking the last box of books. It's one thing to move to a new city, but from Santa Fe at 50,000 people to the southern California megalopolis with 15 million?—that's a magnitude of change that stretches my ability even to envision our actual physical location here, much less a life. But . . . but . . . my great-grandmother, Elizabeth Stevens Lyman, moved here with her husband in 1924 from Kewanne, Illinois. And I was born in La Jolla in 1949, a little more than a hundred miles down the coast. I remember standing in Great-grandmother's living room, young enough to still be shaky on my legs and clutching those white lace curtains downstairs in my right hand while staring out the window, then pointing with my free hand to Wilshire Boulevard and uttering my first word, that quintessential California noun: "Car!" It therefore seems logical that I should be able to anchor myself in Los Angeles among the coordinates of my past, the locations in which my family and I have lived and the drives we've made among them, a thoroughly twentieth-century variation on our longing for an authentic sense of place. I'm connecting up dots in the virtual space-time we inhabit as memory, and the first thing I did after putting up the books was to open that safebox at my feet.

A gray lead-lined container which depends partially on its sheer weight to thwart thieves, it's been pried at by burglars but never broken into, holding secure the diaries and letters, the last wills and testaments of the family collected by my great-grandmother, and then passed on to my mother. Most of the papers are in envelopes bearing Mrs. Lyman's notes to Mom: "Janet, important;" or "Janet: keep." I haul out the box every couple of years to admire its contents: the spidery letters from 1796, farming and manufacturing records from the 1800s, the reams of typed legal-size stock inventories from the 1920s through the 1950s. But now, for the first time, I actually need them, not for an idle rummage through family heritage, but because I'm in Los Angeles, a city that constantly reinvents itself to the world. And I'm lost. So far, the city is simply a location bounded by mountains I mostly can't see, an ocean I can only get to on the weekends, and weak memories of my childhood. These last few two weeks, then, I've spent surveying the past in L.A., fixing down the lines of what must become more than a site *to* me, but a place *for* me.

We moved up the coast from La Jolla in the early summer of 1958, past L.A. to Santa Barbara where my parents' marriage proceeded to fall gloriously and dramatically apart at every seam. Mom and I moved to Reno the next year, where she remarried, and for several Christmas vacations thereafter I flew to Los Angeles, staying with my father's parents at the house in Hollywood. The strongest memories I have of those trips aren't the visits with my father, but of Granddad Fox taking me to the Farmer's Market to shop for vegetables, the same market three blocks away where I now buy my coffee. Their house is about equidistant from our place here and Great-grandmother's, a rough equilateral triangle. My 1996 Gousha Company "Street Map of Los Angeles, Central Section," the most densely gridded piece of paper I've ever seen, is now overlaid with black ink lines of my own after connecting the four locations: Irving Street to Palm Drive to Las Palmas, to our own apartment across from La Brea Tar Pits.

Driving around this morning to peer at the houses, though, was daunting. Mom died before we got around to talking much about these people; so did my father, grandparents, and most of their friends. My ghost houses on this Halloween are marked out on the map in red circles, each linked with black lines running at angles to the predominantly squared-off grid of the city. And while the mapwork does, indeed, help anchor me to what is now a more definable "here," my memories likewise run at a tangent to what should be a linear narrative, the story I wish I could tell myself. Why was my mother so hostile toward her stepmother? And what was he doing in Japan when he died, anyway? My father's family is even more of a mystery. Elbert Marr Fox was born in Mexico, his father an engineer posted there to supervise construction of a bridge; his mother remarried Mac when my father was still a boy. Who was my real paternal grandfather, and what happened to him?

I can't answer those questions or tie down all the loose family ends flapping in the early years of the twentieth century; so, home after my circumnavigation, I continue the survey work. I apply my ruler to another map, one of the United States that I've had since junior high, now cut up so the southwestern states fit on my desk, and upon which I trace a second triangle. The last time I lived in California was in 1967 to go to college in Claremont, just 36 miles to the east over the Covina Hills. My steel ruler stretches from La Jolla, almost at the Mexican border, to Santa Barbara, 180 miles north; from Santa Barbara to Claremont, 117; from Claremont south to La Jolla, 99. We're living in the approximate middle of this triangle, my line on the map from La Jolla to Santa Barbara passing our apartment some nineteen-plus miles out to sea.

When I connect Reno and Santa Fe to these California dots, it reminds me that I've never left the arid lands of the West, even here. L.A. is sometimes identified as the second largest desert city in the world; the 15 million people of the megalopolis between Tijuana and Santa Barbara is roughly equal to, if not as dense as, the population of Cairo, which is ranked first. L.A. sits just over the western edge of the basin-and-range province, and Reno just within that physiographic territory which covers 8 percent of the United States. Its 300,000 square miles even includes Santa Fe on the arid eastern fringe. Reno, Santa Fe, and Los Angeles seem to trade off drought years, and so far this fall it's Los Angeles's turn.

Counting, counting. It's reassuring and grounds me in a constructed matrix of time and space. It's the concatenation of the two in that ephemeral set of cranial algorithms we call memory that turns location into place. I echo-locate myself within that constellation of great-uncles and grandparents, reading aloud the family records written by Great-grandmother Lyman, a short ferocious woman who dressed entirely in black and who would check my mother's lipstick at night for smears when my parents were dating.

Before putting away the ruler, I make one last set of measurements: Reno to Santa Fe, the course of the one move, roughly 792 straight-line miles; then Santa Fe to Los Angeles, 720; Los Angeles to Reno, 396. Las Vegas lies inside the triangle, close enough to the middle to satisfy me. I'm not seeking mathematical symmetry, but metaphor: my map is only the earth's curved surface projected awkwardly onto a flat sheet by the National Geographic Society; and, my steel ruler is less than perfectly precise. Besides, geomancy isn't really my point. "**Geomancy . . .** divination by random figures formed when a handful of earth is cast on the ground, or by dots or lines drawn at random." Great-grandmother would, I believe, nod approvingly over the box beneath my feet, her carefully annotated records preserved for my two sons; but, as a midwestern Presbyterian, she definitely would not have approved of my going so far as to attempt divination of either my past or future from triangles drawn on a map.

Sunday, November 10

The weather here is impossibly devoted to seasonal invariance. Summer should be long gone and autumn half-past, and though a foot of snow clings above the ten-thousand-foot level on Mt. Baldy in the San Gabriels—just fifty miles away and sweetly visible from any freeway in town—it's 94 degrees downtown, 80 at the beach, and a half-dozen dolphins cruise just outside the breakers as we body surf in the two-foot shore break. The smog's blown out to sea the last three days, its brown residue all but obscuring the ridgetops of Catalina and Santa Cruz islands. Directly above us in the Malibu foothills are 13,000 or so acres charred by a wildfire a few weeks ago, millions of tons of topsoil poised to wash into the Pacific this winter. North America continues to rise along its western edge, and a wide part of its Pacific continental shelf

d grounds me in a constructed matrix of time and space.

extends here, beneath our feet as we tread water. The Palos Verdes Peninsula, visible to the south today, is the fastest rising piece of ground on the planet, and Mt. Baldy a principal crown atop the steepest range in America, which is busy both building itself up and tearing itself down in a frenzy of geological terrorism against the city. If it's not earthquakes up-thrusting the mountainsides, it's erosion washing them down over hillside neighborhoods and onto the growing undersea shelf.

In the meantime, everything is quiet this fall now that the fire season is over. The Santa Ana winds are still blowing from the east—that's why we can see Baldy and the smog is blanketing Catalina instead of San Bernardino this week—but they're late enough in the year that they're coming from cooler weather over the Great Basin instead of late summer heat. Impossibly nice. No season at all. Not hot or cold, the sun just a little too low even at midday to pose a serious threat of sunburn. The dolphins arc slowly in pairs beside the surfers to our left.

Back on the beach to dry off, Beth settles in with the *Los Angeles Times,* which this Sunday features an article on the renovation of Hollywood and the Sunset Strip, the massive leveraging of private capital in the hundreds of millions of dollars against the tattoo parlors, t-shirt shops, and prostitutes. It's a historical landmark district less than a century old, yet fallen into decrepitude, laments a resident. Thirty years ago Reyner Banham, the architectural historian, pointed out that Hollywood had floresced over only two decades during the first half of the twentieth century, and had been declining in civic fact, if not the collective imagination of America, ever since. My thoughts this afternoon have to do with the three family houses, the architectural styles of Los Angeles and Las Vegas, and how fantasy connects the two cities. The fantasy is based in the nature of the landscape here, Los Angeles at the western end of the Mojave Desert, Las Vegas at the eastern. It's more triangulation, tying my personal memories to how we remember ourselves collectively within our society through architecture.

According to the aerial photos in the Page Museum over at the Tar Pits, Great-grandmother's house on Irving Street must have been about on the leading edge of the urban Los Angeles grid, which wouldn't reach out farther west to encapsulate our neighborhood for almost another decade. Her house is a restatement of midwestern virtue, albeit on the generous side of the residential scale and with some decorative touches. Grandfather Lyman's house, while demonstrating a businessman's foursquare seriousness, celebrates its location in a climate more Mediterranean than that of central Illinois. If eclectic, it nonetheless alludes to the Romanesque villa architecture of southern Europe.

Mac's house falls within that Spanish-style spectrum of arched doorways and tiled roofs which includes the house I grew up in above La Jolla, as well as the Santa Barbara residence where my father dissolved his marriage in a series of affairs I sometimes glimpsed through half-closed windows. It's a residential fashion based romantically around the conceits and embellishments of the Spanish missions, refined in the early twentieth century by architect Reginald Johnson into what's called "Casa California," where southwestern adobe meets the Riviera. At its best, it can appear endlessly elegant while gracefully hiding the sins of structural boredom, and is in my mind thus perfectly suited to marital infidelity. At its worst, it's merely pasteurized Spanish Colonial Revival, the most pervasive manifestation of stucco since its invention in Egypt several millennia ago. The style and the technology first met in the Southern California of the 1950s, when developers realized how quick and easy the two made a subdivision possible, and the combination has become by far the dominant residential motif from Los Angeles to Phoenix.

Rolling over in the sand from my speculations, during which I've taken to biting my fingernails as I replay the memory of architecture and parental divorce, I can now scan the houses left naked from the fires on the slopes above. As always, I'm wishing for the binoculars, but even from the beach I can catalog the residential follies. In addition to three-story Spanish minimansions, we have Glorified Vernacular Beachhouse in weathered clapboard, Cape Cod Summer Home, and Postindustrial Ranchette. While the film industry busily assembles storybook environments inside studios larger than airplane hangers, and on surreal backlots where the Wild West cohabits with Al Capone's Chicago, all of it is overshadowed by this routine construction of fantasy by the upper middle class.

Banham makes the point in his seminal book about Southern California, *Los Angeles: The Architecture of Four Ecologies,* which I have on the towel beside me, that the process of usurping architectural styles to display status and wealth has gone further in Las Vegas than here, but that it was Hollywood that first brought together the unique mix of diverse artistic and construction talents able to translate personal ego into residential monuments. Banham passed away in 1988, just before the renewed round of surreality on the Las Vegas Strip, and I wonder what he would have written about it. Despite the restaurants here shaped like hot dogs and derby hats, and Chinese theaters and Mayan nightclubs, Los Angeles has mostly concentrated its architectural excess in residential glorification of the personal, whereas Las Vegas has made it democratically commercial, what the art critic Jeff Kelley, who was raised in Las Vegas, once called "the American Dream in drag."

Some simple comparisons will do. The most expensive purchase on record of an American residence is David Geffen's Beverly Hills house; for $47.5 million he received a neoclassical mansion on ten acres that contains an imported wood floor said to be that upon which Napoleon proposed to Josephine. Aaron Spelling, who lives in the same neighborhood as the Playboy mansion, just built a house of 123 rooms that runs to 56,000 square feet ($51 million). Los Angeles has the largest number of high-end residential properties of any city in the country, and Las Vegas is not even close to being in the same class. It does, however, build the world's largest hotels, five-and six-thousand-room behemoths financed with billion-dollar lines of credit. The combined debt service and operating costs means the attached casinos must clear over a million dollars per day. Las Vegas can't rely upon just the gamblers of America to meet such demands, but must instead market itself to the larger "family travel" crowd seeking "entertainment." Architectural spectacles with attendant amusements are in order.

Pointing out that Las Vegas in the 1950s was mostly "an extreme suburban variant" of Los Angeles, with motels in Nevada simply adding big signs and bland industrial buildings to serve as casinos, Banham derided the construction of Caesar's Palace in 1967 as "boring Beaux-Arts." He was certainly entitled and qualified to utter such a judgment, but Caesar's led the movement that turned Las Vegas inside out, pulling off a reversal of field-to-ground that's become its signature. Where the Las Vegas skyline used to comprise solely the world's largest signs towering above the Strip, inviting customers to step inside the unassuming warehouses of gaming behind the ubiquitous parking lots, now the buildings have become the signs themselves. The buildings that used to be in the background have assumed the foreground figure of the signs. So, while the bedroom streets of Las Vegas are for the most part numbingly repetitious two- and three-bedroom variations on the aforementioned Spanish Colonial theme, the economic engine of Las Vegas is clad in oversized fantasies outclassing, mile by mile, any other streets in the world. It would have come as a reassurance to Banham and his Hollywood thesis that Las Vegas relies heavily upon cadres of designers lured away from Disney and other studios in Los Angeles to make real its wet concrete dreams.

It's not that I don't like L.A.; I do, and the reason why is related to the nature of Las Vegas, which I also admire, despite abysmally deep misgivings: Both are cities exercising the complete will to imagination. What started out on the Sunset Strip in 1927, with its twenty-five-bungalow Garden of Allah hotel, simply followed the road east until it found the largest and most conveniently located piece of emptiness available; within twenty years it had metamorphosed into the Flamingo. What is it about the arid West, if not the outright desert, that leads us to such indulgence?

Gaston Bachelard says of distance in the landscape that we miniaturize and then imaginatively possess that which is far but still visible. We envision ourselves inhabiting that mountain in the distance, the far shore of the lake as we cruise by, the small town at the end of a handsome valley just in view off the interstate. There are no distances on land any more insistent than those of the American Southwest, in particular as we come overland to Los Angeles or Las Vegas. It doesn't matter if we drive, fly, or walk; we're surrounded by in-your-face and stretching-as-far-as-the-eye-can-see, clichéd-and-stereotyped, *distance.* We arrive in these cities having already exercised our fantasy of possession to an extreme degree. Our sense of habitation, if we're not worrying about details of the journey such as running out of water or cash, is liberated. Anything goes. And we'll build a house or a casino to prove it!

There's much that's been said about our sense of freedom in the West, and how it relates to everything from nineteenth-century hubris to sheer twentieth-century economic exhilaration, but it's also an expansive habit of mind based directly on the landscape. Some would have it that we left behind common sense and good taste as we moved West in the early twentieth century. We approached and wound our way through range upon range of jagged peaks, the desert air so dry that not a single outline was blurred even forty miles away. The mountains looked so close we almost stopped the car to walk up the nearest ridge for a view. Our imagination wandered to visions of castles. We crossed the Mojave Desert and seemed to jettison family traditions and the architectural conventions of established suburbs in the East and Midwest.

When we settled down to build a house in Los Angeles, we allowed ourselves to externalize that gothic mansion held over from our childhood, the romantic fairytale cottage, the pink dollhouse—whatever it took to extend outwards our egos and skins, if you will. The middle class arriving then in Los Angeles brought with it an already thriving American appetite for residential revivalism, a period when Georgian, Victorian, Edwardian, and Colonial houses were built next to each other on most every well-to-do residential street in the country. After surviving what was still an adventurous crossing of the Great American Desert, imaginations were further liberated. There was also no pre-existing cohesive civic identity here, so everyone ran off in their own direction, precisely part of the reason they'd come here in the first place. The fact that the movies were a major economic staple of the town only added to the sense of fun: Let's not leave our fantasies on the silver screen, let's live in them! And as the movies were themselves often filmed in local houses, the residential fantasies were made public, were celebrated, and therefore validated by audiences, a self-reinforcing cycle that continues today. As architect Alan Hess, who used to teach at UCLA, has pointed out, contemporary or experimental residential architecture in the West continues to exist on a fantasy level all its own, the most extreme of which he's labeled "Hyperwest."

In some ways this can be an architecture without many pretenses (though it can be pretentious). As art critic Dave Hickey, formerly of Los Angeles and now happily of Las Vegas, once noted during a talk given in Santa Fe (here liberally paraphrased): In Las Vegas no one really thinks the Luxor is an Egyptian tomb, or Caesar's Palace a place where Roman gladiators lounge around eating peeled grapes; everyone takes those fantasies for what they are. In Santa Fe, however, almost every tourist takes for real adobe the stucco-and-frame construction mandated by city regulations to imitate adobe—the same stucco construction used in Las Vegas subdivisions which, for the most part, look exactly like the contemporary tract houses for casino workers that they in fact are.

How I feel about moving to Los Angeles falls somewhere between chronic un-ease and the more acute state of dis-ease, a discomfort requiring conscious acts of will, such as ruling triangles on the map, at least to mitigate if not overcome my floating anxiety. Amidst the extremes of movie-mansion ghettos, and the mind-numbing square miles of red-tile roofs, how do I know where I am? Where do I place my memory?

Writing down the family addresses, connecting them first on paper and then on pavement, are attempts to invest Los Angeles with personal memory, to stabilize a manageable portion of local geography in my imagination. Because the family landscape is in Los Angeles, an extended city designed *de facto* by automobile, it can only be perceived as an integrated whole by driving. The entire West, as a matter of fact, is like that. We can't walk from town to town to assemble a view of it, but have to fly over it, or even better, drive it in order to understand it.

I lived in Reno for thirty-three years, moving from California when young enough to switch allegiance and count myself a Nevadan. When moving to Santa Fe, I conceived of myself as becoming a New Mexican. Leaving Santa Fe to live in Los Angeles leaves me very confused: Am I a native Californian? A footloose Nevadan forever circling the Great Basin? A westerner just hopping from town to town? Documenting the drives to Las Vegas helps me to assimilate the larger territory; counting my way around is a means to force the question out into the open, and to transform location into place. I'm used to having deep and specific roots—staying in one place for over three decades will do that—and living in a city where the architecture is no more stable than the hillsides above us is deeply unsettling.

Writing down the family addresses . . . are attempts to invest Los Angeles with person

High clouds are now moving in, lowering the beach temperature by maybe a degree or two, and we pack it in for the day, joining the stream of Harley-Davidsons, the ever-present black wedges of Mercedes and Lexi, the topless Jeeps, and vintage Mustangs as they cruise down the Pacific Coast Highway and into Santa Monica. I'm torn between counting Ferraris and reading the small neon street signs on houses facing the beach, which present to the highway only their garage doors and otherwise unadorned backsides. Neon street numbers. That's a new one, adopting the street signage of the Strip for the Pacific Coast Highway. We curve up and left through a tunnel, leaving the ocean to join Interstate 10 where it begins—or, were I sitting in its other terminus, Jacksonville, Florida, where I would say it ends. In either case, it's the freeway we'll use to start our trip to Las Vegas in eleven days.

Sunday, November 17

I'm setting out the maps, notebooks, pens, and, yes, the binoculars for the trip on Thursday, still thinking about the Southwest and fantasy. There were several reasons behind the exploration of the region from the 1500s through the 1850s, aside from the sheer momentum of western expansionism which wasn't going to end until it ran up against something it couldn't subdivide, like the Pacific Ocean. The search for fur-bearing beaver, and the competition among the French, English, and then the Americans to establish trade routes to Asia were two important ones; but an overarching drive common throughout the era of exploration was the quest for treasure, specifically gold.

The Spanish marched up from Mexico in a series of disastrous expeditions for centuries, following the myth of the Seven Cities of Cibola and rumors of a legendary river, the San Buenaventura. The American explorers believed much of the geographical lore handed down from the Spanish, and if not al-

emory, to stabilize a manageable portion of local geography in my imagination.

ways convinced there were lost tribes beating out platters of gold, they were pretty sure there was an as-yet undiscovered river leading to either vast herds of beaver, an economical trade route to China, unspecified natural riches, or all three. It wasn't until John Frémont in 1843–44 circumnavigated the Great Basin, the last unexplored region in the continental United States, that a large enough array of survey points was amassed to disprove the notion of the San Buenaventura. But by then the fantastical allure of mystery and wealth was irrevocably embedded in the psyche of the Southwest. When Great-grandmother moved here in 1924, she was just one of the million people who migrated to L.A. that decade in search of a better life—the fabled weather and limitless opportunities. At least they had the first part right.

Las Vegas was an oasis, literally, on the Old Spanish Trail from Santa Fe to Los Angeles, a route which had first been established in the late 1700s by friars seeking to connect the missions and oceanic supply lines of the two regions. By the mid-1880s the route was the most heavily used overland passage in the Southwest, part of which had become known as the Mormon Trail for the emigrants coming down from Utah on their way to California. The Gold Rush and the 1860s boom of the Comstock Lode in Nevada did nothing but reinforce the idea that the entire point of Westward Ho! was to fulfill one's dreams of untold riches. It's no wonder that fantasy is the prevalent building code of the region, and its architecture Spanish Colonial Revival, a commercial romanticization of everyman's *casa grande.*

On top of the historical lust for treasure, every nightmare you ever had about its contemporary relative, rampant consumerism, has found its ultimate expression here, whether it's the Rolls Royces and minks of Beverly Hills, the lavish parties and weddings of movie stars, or simply the generation of 4,000 tons of solid residential waste daily. (Not only is Los Angeles a big city, it uses and discards more waste weekly than some entire countries.) The consumerism is based, in turn, on desire, as if by purchasing and using and eating enough varieties of experience we'll achieve enlightenment: The purpose of the universe will come clear if only we buy enough of it, or we'll have a good time trying. It doesn't matter if you're American, Mexican, Laotian, or Ukrainian: Los Angeles is the place to come find your fortune, your bliss, your dream house with a jacuzzi.

Christopher Knight, one of America's great art critics, who writes for the *Los Angeles Times,* points out the psychic faultline in all this: "The city of colossal dreams and endless promise that's always in the ascendant, Los Angeles is also notorious for never quite being able to make it over the top, for repeatedly failing to make the grade. The Sisyphean paradox is this: Wretched failure is perversely essential to mass culture's whopping triumphs. Desire is the fuel that turns the engines of consumption, and relentless disappointment is what generates perpetual desire."

It's scary, our literal and emotional economies looped through desires that can't be fulfilled, our disappointment leading us to buy onward only to be let down again, which sounds suspiciously like the psychology of western migration (the grass is always greener . . .). Las Vegas is the architectural and financial apotheosis of this cycle, and how convenient it is that the historical oasis was waiting just across the desert to be converted into L.A.'s playroom. And, because as goes Los Angeles so goes California and the nation, we have gambling metastasizing in New Jersey, in Mississippi, in New Mexico. . . .

When I was in my twenties I worked the graveyard shift at Harold's Club in Reno in the "prime count" room, where all the coins not paid back to slot machine players were brought in buckets stacked in wheeled carts to be counted. The contents of each bucket were poured into a tray on a digital scale, and the number of the slot machine from which the coins had been taken entered into the computer, which then converted the weight into monetary value and compared the take to the statistical payout average to which the machine had been set. It was an efficient, though noisy, method of counting money while checking the security of the individual slot machines.

Despite using earplugs, I'm slightly deaf from the excruciating clamor of nickels, dimes, quarters, and silver dollars as they were dumped down a steel chute to the vault in the basement where they were counted again (ensuring none of us were involved in our own take), then rolled, sent up the elevator in another cart, and sold back to customers the same day!

It was a perpetual money machine in metaphor, if not in exact fact: *After* the customers had raked in their paybacks of anywhere from 93 to 98 percent of what they put into the slots, the take we counted every twenty-four hours coming out of Harold's Club's 900-plus machines sometimes exceeded

$125,000. The ratio of payback to the customers was much lower at the table games and, of course, much more lucrative for the club. Clark County, home to Las Vegas, currently hosts more than 110,000 slot machines, many of them located on the ground floors of the mega-resorts, which helps explain how they make their debt payments.

I remain amazed at the massive elegance and simplicity of that cash operation and the willing participation of patrons, but thanks to Knight I now have a larger context in which to exercise my awe. It's not just the possibility of winning, but also the disappointment which we know the odds are set to provide us, that keep us coming back to the table. Gambling is a very unadorned cycle of consumerism, the cultivation of desire and subsequent devouring of our own disappointment. It's not gambling that's the addiction, but consumption of which gambling is just a symptom. That also helps explain why Banham found the buildings in Las Vegas to be a glorified extension of L.A.'s commercial architecture. It's all rose-tinted smoke and one-way mirrors lined up along the streets of both cities, the difference being that Las Vegas is designed to revel overtly in its consumerist excellence, exactly the naked intent that Dave Hickey admires.

Los Angeles is a city we envision as having banks, department stores, and residential suburbs, so we have mixed feelings about the public display of excessive consumption in its commercial architectural. And, in fact, L.A.'s commercial architecture has, since Banham wrote his book about the city, gone first through a phase of Japanese-financed modernism, the tidy black boxes on Wilshire Boulevard marching along like conservative business suits, and then a sporadic bout of postmodernism with its witty self-references and historical quotes. L.A.'s commercial architecture is downright puritanical compared to the Strip's. Las Vegas is our commercial sandbox, the beach of our collective imagination, and public castles are the order of the day. While the private house designs in L.A. grow ever more hyper, the reverse is true in Las Vegas, where the gated ghettos of the rich are as monotonous as the service tunnels beneath Disneyland. Its residential architecture tends not to express wealth by style, but by size—the houses of the upper class are usually just bigger versions of the colonial suburbs.

The road to Las Vegas takes many forms, but the one from L.A. is the fastest and most direct. In literal fact, it parallels roughly the route of the Spanish missionaries from over two centuries ago, as well as the railroad, the trading paths of Paiute and Mojave Indians, and their paleolithic ancestors. In metaphor, it's as if the motels and clubs on Sunset Strip in the 1930s had simply migrated eastward to a winter home in the desert, caught a little too much radiation from the atomic bomb tests nearby, and mutated into mega(ton) resorts of the Las Vegas Strip.

Interstate 15, the contemporary route which Beth and I will take, also retraces the drive my parents took in May of 1934, when they snuck out of the house on Irving Street and eloped to Las Vegas to be married. Their bid for freedom didn't do them much good; the Depression kept them living with Great-grandmother in her spacious home on Irving Street, where she continued to terrorize my mother each night before bed, taking Mom's chin in her hands and tilting it up in the light to check her lipstick. While I wouldn't exactly call our drive to Las Vegas a stroll down memory lane, it holds both the key to how the two cities relate to each other, and yet one more clue to the construction of memory at the end of the millennium.

TWO

Thursday, November 21, 7:20 A.M.

We're running later than we would have liked this morning, a complicated feeling given that it's raining. We both hate leaving town and missing the storm, but traffic will already be bad. If we're lucky, we won't drive completely out of it; rain is a highly desirable state in which to introduce Beth to the Mojave. Her first decision is to take surface streets into downtown before picking up the freeway, which means we'll avoid most of the commuter mess. The odometer is once again set to zero, and we're at 265 miles from the edge of Las Vegas. I surround myself with maps, the infamous binoculars, even an altimeter. I could get used to this.

The slightly cartoonish logo at the top of the twenty-five-story Entertainment Television building over on Wilshire is buried in low clouds as we turn onto 6th, and the sound of tires on wet pavement for the first time since we've been in L.A. is reassuring. Weather still does, after all, exist! We pass Irving Street and a few minutes later MacArthur Park which is, just like the song from twenty-five years ago, "melting in the rain." (A disadvantage to memory in L.A. is that, as one of the world's mythical cities, pop culture invades your reveries with readymade images). A solitary jogger pegs his way around the lake, presumably freed by the inclement weather from the drug dealers who normally claim the park these days as home turf. With the skyscrapers of downtown cut off by fog around the twenty-five-story level, the radio reporting 61 degrees and no traffic accidents, Beth performs something that resembles aerial acrobatics to lift us up from the surface grid to, first, the 110 southbound, and then quickly onto Interstate 10 east. It's not a particularly easy maneuver in the rain, and the last time I tried it in clear weather we ended up halfway to Long Beach on the 110 before I could get turned around.

Traffic is pretty light in our direction, though it's at a crawl going opposite us into downtown. The slow number one lane is packed with semi's and there's even water in the oversize concrete gutter that's the Los Angeles River. Paralleling the river is what's known here as the Santa Ana Freeway, the local stretch of Interstate 5 which links the Mexican and Canadian borders. The 5 isn't a pretty freeway, just multiple lanes leveled at the fastest passage from one agribusiness district to another in the central valleys of California, Oregon, and Washington; but still, it's noteworthy, this crossing over another major continental arterial. We pass the Forest Lawn Cemetery on our right, graveyard workers dressed in cheerful yellow slickers surrounding a backhoe performing their own maneuvers of passage, and then we're approaching one of the best pieces of public architecture in all of Los Angeles County. I put away the Gousha city map and actually enjoy the massive vehicular slow-down as we enter the 605 interchange.

The 605 starts here at the foot of the San Gabriel Mountains and follows the San Gabriel River as it flows south into the Pacific just below Long Beach. I find it remarkable that an urban structure devoted exclusively to autotopia actually flows with the natural geography, such as it is, instead of ignoring it. The San Gabriel fares only slightly better than its sister the Los Angeles River in freedom of movement. To our right is one of the numerous and enormous reservoirs and flood basins placed along its path, a reminder that the word "*natural*" should never be used lightly in L.A. The interchange itself is one of those near-archtypal science fiction visions common to those of us who grew up in the 1950s watching Jetson cartoons on Saturday mornings—another readymade. Its six overpasses and three tiers of recrossing traffic in the light rain is almost that future we sincerely believed in forty years ago, one in which people would drive off through the sky to work without fear of vehicular or cardiac congestion. The interchange is massive and glorious, not big enough to reach the industrial sublime level of, say, Hoover Dam, but still impressive.

As we idle foot by foot under the concrete spans, however, Beth points out a jagged crack in the pavement in front of us, a shallow lightning-like split you could fit a couple of fingers into that runs for many yards and across two lanes. It's easily the longest crack in a road we've ever seen anywhere. Remnant of an earthquake, she speculates? Clever thought while we're underneath several thousand tons of cement and rebar. Our cartoon dreams of progress always have their dark side. The crack and the floods, the river and the freeway, the collision of land and city: each juxtaposition brings into play another meaning of fantasy as applied to our built environment, this one an awareness that the ultimate architectural folly is one that leads us to believe we're in control for more than a moment or two. We may flatten and stabilize the surface landscape, but the land beneath has its own agenda.

While mulling over such properly gloomy thoughts for a rainy morning, I'm also keeping track of the pod we're traveling in. There's a compact sedan filled with party balloons, which must make for interesting lane changes, a blue pickup carrying a stack of two-by-fours flagged at the end, a red mini-van, a blue Tercel, and at 8:07 A.M. a white Cadillac with a guy smoking a cigar. This only reinforces my undeniable prejudice against Cadillacs—I like cigars once a year, but at eight in the morning with the windows rolled up?—there's something wrong with these people. Time to pull out a new map, the legendary AAA version of San Bernardino County.

In an 1854 map of the New Mexico Province, Rio Arriba County is shown as stretching from the Rio Grande Valley to the Colorado River, virtually from Santa Fe to Las Vegas, the entire length of my drive in the previous essay. San Bernardino County doesn't reach quite that far—and neither does New Mexico these days, Arizona having since been created in between—but the 1996 version of the AAA San Bernardino County map starts at Claremont and spans the Mojave clear to the Colorado River, running over the borders of both Nevada and Arizona. At twenty thousand square miles, San Bernardino is the largest county in the United States and includes parts of the Death Valley and Joshua Tree national parks, all of the Mojave National Preserve, chunks of the China Lake Naval Weapons Center and Edwards Air Force Base, as well as the entirety of the army's Fort Irwin National Training Center and the Marine Corps Air Ground Combat Center in the Bullion Mountains. This piece of white paper with its ten creases now unfolded over my side of the car covers roughly 140.8 by 214.4 miles, or about 30,185 square miles of the driest, hottest, most well-traveled, explored, and filmed desert in the Western Hemisphere. (I'd say "the world," but Libya holds the world's record temperature for heat since 1922, at 136 degrees, one degree fahrenheit hotter than the

Death Valley record; and several deserts, including parts of the Sahara, are drier than the Mojave's annual rainfall, which averages 4.52 inches annually.)

8:16 A.M. When I was a kid the AAA map would have shown Death Valley and Joshua Tree to be national monuments, not parks. The military bases were already there in the 1950s, but the freeways were only on the drawing boards, and the high plateau that would be set aside in the 1990s as the Mojave National Preserve was still open territory for miners, ranchers, prophets, and a place for organized crime to dump bodies. What the map demonstrates this morning is a relentless encroachment of the urban grid east from Los Angeles and deep into the desert.

The space between Los Angeles and Las Vegas, even when I was in college, was mostly just that: space. The megalopolis used to stop at San Bernardino, but it's now leapfrogged the San Gabriel and San Bernardino mountains to spread its streets and commuter suburbs out to the edge of the wilderness areas north of Joshua Tree and the once remote military bases. Some of the 20-mph westbound traffic that Beth and I are passing at quarter after eight this morning left driveways in the Mojave an hour before sunrise in order to be on time for work in Los Angeles. I have another cartographic resource in the car, the oversized *Southern & Central California Atlas & Gazetteer* published by DeLorme Mapping in 1990, a book which contains topographic maps of our route and confirms the malignancy of the grid in bright orange for housing and red lines for streets.

The infill between L.A. and Las Vegas is astonishing. Water is so scarce it's almost comic, the heat and wind relentless enough to strip the paint off your car in a year, most jobs and services a hundred-mile or more roundtrip. The more I look at the map, the less sense it makes and the more disturbed I get. There's such a natural cutoff for urban spread at the mountains that it seems totally illogical to have built beyond them, to have violated what the map graphically represents as what could have been a pristine area of clear paper.

We hit the interchange with Interstate 15 and a few minutes later the 215 joins in with another great set of flying buttresses. There's now thick fog outside, and simultaneously a flurry of paper inside that Beth is valiantly trying to keep on my side of the car; her visibility extends maybe 300 yards out the window and about six inches in the Honda. I close the atlas and fold the AAA map in half to avoid becoming a statistic on the morning traffic report, and am just in time to read the first sign for Las Vegas. We're 214 miles out, running north by northeast at just under a thousand feet above sea level, and beginning the climb into Cajon Canyon. It occurs to me that, because I'm not driving, I'm spending too much time looking at maps and not enough actually watching where we're going.

Beth concentrates on the accelerating traffic, now up to 65 mph, and I start counting lines in the landscape parallel to our freeway lane, long horizontals which have been visually isolated by the fog. I lose track at thirty-six. The most noticeable ones, aside from ten lanes of pavement, are the powerlines and the railroad. The powerlines come from Hoover Dam, and we'll follow them over the Nevada border where they take a bend to the right across a dry lake bed, disappearing over the mountains and into the lower reaches of Black Canyon. Railroad tracks will come and go all along our route, the Union Pacific clear up into Nevada, but the Atchison, Topeka, Santa Fe diverging east at Barstow, where it follows the Mojave River in a more easterly direction toward Needles.

The robotic high tension towers march up the canyon with us, as well as a train with what looks to be a hundred cars being bullied up the tracks by seven engines. At 3,400 feet the fog thickens into soup and everyone on the road slows to under 60, a major concession to safety on a California freeway. Go too fast and we'll rear-end the semi-truck passing another in our lane; go too slow and we'll be flattened by the white consumer-electronics delivery van behind us.

At 186 miles from Las Vegas the road levels off at 4,260 feet, then dips

The architecture of the Mojave favors one-story prefab . . . bulldozed through th slightly down while the clouds lift sharply upwards; the floor of the Mojave Desert stretches out before us for sixty or seventy miles. Beth is blown away by our first clear line of sight over land since moving to L.A. three months ago, and when she finally looks down to check her speed she's going over 90. Nothing like a little open space to get the blood going. Bill Barker, an artist and ex-Angeleno now hunkered down in Reno, once told me that the drive up Cajon Pass was like decompressing from the deep sea. This morning it does feel that reaching the Mojave is like breaching the surface of the planet, and Barker would appreciate the way the clouds behind us are breaking over the San Bernardinos, enormous combers of rain curling over the mountains and into the Big Empty of the desert.

The map, to which I can't help referring, is telling a different story: it's not empty. The red grid spiderwebs its way all over the atlas page, everything for miles marked off in squares, and the town of Hesperia to our right glows orange on paper next to the freeway line. What's changed is mostly the density of habitation, and after a few minutes our eyes adjust to a new depth of focal detail. The architecture of the Mojave favors one-story prefab, and the streets are just dirt, bulldozed through the creosote with intersections marked by occasional slightly absurd fire hydrants. Just east of Victorville, through which the Mojave River could almost be described as flowing this morning from runoff in the mountains, there's a brand-new development of two-story Spanish Colonial apartments. I can't decide who's suffering more here, the apartment dwellers who have to look at the mobile homes next door with their ubiquitous ring of abandoned vehicles, or the locals who hauled their possessions up here to be away from exactly this suburban clone.

Far off to the right there's a high berm shoved up against a line of hills, the front edge of a cyanide pond that's slowly leaching out microscopic gold from old tailings. I make myself giddy scanning the landscape through the binoculars for the dozens of mines shown on the maps. For a desert this is the most intensely worked-over terrain I can imagine. Car, truck, RV, dirt bike, and other ATV tracks are everywhere, as are the churned paths of heavy mining equipment.

At mile 161.5 the freeway turns red, as if it were imitating the map, its paving material matching the color of the hills being shredded by bulldozers, a shade which Beth tentatively labels rose aubergine. I'm admiring the dense land fog that's settled in over Brisbane Valley to the north when Beth precisely twitches the steering wheel to avoid a dog that runs full tilt into the road. Seventy-five pounds of canine does a backwards airborne somersault, jerked to safety, though probably not with an entirely intact spine, by a guy dressed in camouflage on the other end of the leash. I watch in the mirror as the guy stuffs his dog into the camper shell on the back of his pickup, one of three stopped on the edge of the shoulder. This is still a freeway out here, but people treat it as if it's your backyard country road, with often fatal results.

Passing mile 148.5, our adrenaline abated, there's an exit sign for Outlet Center Drive. Never mind there's not yet a building in sight, but at least we're almost prepared when we top the rise in front of us and confront "100 Factory Outlet Stores," arrayed in full Spanish-you-know-what splendor. Nothing's open this early in the morning, but we're within an hour of San Bernardino; I can only imagine what the traffic will be like a week from now on the busiest shopping day of the year. No one's going to be clipping along at the 75–80 mph that Beth's struggling to limit us to as we roll down into Barstow.

9:30 A.M. We've promised ourselves a coffee break and spend fifteen minutes at MacDonald's stretching, then wolfing down a breakfast in lieu of the one we should have had at home. When I was a kid driving back and forth from Claremont to Reno on breaks during college, Barstow was one of the places I'd stop for gas and then turn left to link up with US 395. I still call that highway the most beautiful drive in America, a road that runs up out of the low desert to trace the entire flank of the eastern Sierra Nevada, an escarpment that thrusts up 10,000 vertical feet next to your left shoulder. Barstow was always filled with wind-borne sand, a gritty place to stop; the wind is still here and it's safer to eat inside than out.

Barstow is a key intersection in the triangulation I began on October 15, when I first sat down with map and ruler. This marks where I-40 ends, where that dense truck flow from Albuquerque turns south, following the Mojave River to Victorville, and then dives down Cajon Pass into the megalopolis. Second, it's one of the intersections for the turn north to Reno. Third, it's where I-15 bends east for Las Vegas, the traffic more recreational in nature than I-40 and composed mostly of cars. To look at Barstow on the San Bernardino County map is to locate immediately the single most obvious nexus of roads in the region. It's also where, once we leave the MacDonald's parking lot, the past starts to feel more tangible to me, as if I'm driving literally backwards into time, guided there by these geographical associations.

Back on the road at 9:47, altitude around 2,400 feet. Two and a half miles out of town there's road construction and an electric sign proclaiming "Left lane Flooded." We slow down enough to read the separate red and blue graffiti on the highway dividers, signal colors of the rival Crips and Bloods from L.A., but there's no standing water anywhere. There is, however, a California Highway Patrol car on the other side of the construction with two cars pulled over, only the second cop we've seen this morning. Beth modestly accelerates past, reminding herself to stay light on the pedal. Seven billboards for Las Vegas casinos beckon us onward, the first we've seen.

We're now following the northern side of the Mojave Valley, which contains the last major agriculture until the lawns of Las Vegas, and Beth asks me if the desert is like this all the way to Nevada, filled with gas stations and greenhouses, shopping malls and fast food joints. Soon, I say, soon it changes; but first we have three very interesting sights next to us. To the right is the Yermo U.S. Marine Corps Logistics Base, acre after acre of warehouses, bunkers, and so many trucks and tanks lined up that even with both of us counting we can't estimate the number of rows, much less the individual vehicles, as we pass. I want to stop for a tally but am too embarrassed, either by thought of being taken for a spy or a right-wing weapons fanatic. The vehicles—thousands of Humvees, Bradleys, tanks, and fuel trucks—are painted in either basic fatigue green or basic sand, a base coat awaiting application of the appropriate camouflage for wooded terrain or another Desert Storm.

The military presence throughout the basin and range is considerable, from the Atomic Test Site in southern Nevada to the China Lake Naval Weapons Center next to 395. Driving through the desert gives us a glimpse of army tanks as they crawl across the valley floors ten miles away, chasing each other like prehistoric beetles under a surreal canopy of pink flares. It affords us the momentary pleasure of being buzzed by low-flying fighters as they use the car roof for laser targeting practice, and being stuck behind lumbering flatbed trucks carrying dangerous-looking hulks wrapped in black tarpaulins. The military requires large spaces in which to exercise, preferably ones where they can lay out strategy on a board clearly visible to their observers, yet tucked out of range from prolonged civilian inspection. Hence my shyness about stopping. I've been buzzed enough while hiking through bombing ranges in Nevada, armed soldiers hanging out the open doors of helicopters with cameras.

10:12 A.M. A billboard for the Stardust suggests politely that we "Enter the Night!" at 126.7 miles out from Las Vegas as we pass the Minneola Road exit. Far across the valley an array of a hundred and fifty–plus rows of solar panels winks briefly in the intermittent sunlight, clouds pursuing us as the storm tracks inland. The desert encourages us to line up, to deploy massive and simple geometries—Marine Corps troop carriers, hothouse vegetables, solar collectors, everything parallel to each other, a vast outdoor storage shelf. To our left there's a different kind of storage activity, another set of highly visible and anomalous behaviors.

The Calico Mountains top out at just over 4,500 feet, about 2,100 feet above us, more a cluster of steep and varicolored hills than real peaks. Numerous mines dot the area, the ever-present extractive industriousness of mankind still on open display here. But in one corner of a small draw there's another one of those huge berms, a clean-edged earthwork several yards high and bounded at the bottom by a fence tall enough to catch stray flyballs or, in this case, stray wastepaper. It's a landfill, though, not a mine or a ballfield, and it's situated next to an archeological dig that might contain the earliest evidence of man in the Western Hemisphere. On the one hand we're laying down the garbage of L.A. as layers of evidence for future scientists, and on the other we're excavating the past of the region just as deeply.

The Calico Early Man Site figures heavily in my thoughts about the prehistory of the West and its deserts, partly because one of my best friends in college, the writer Bruce McAllister, was so excited about it even then. To make a genuinely long story short, which is tough for numerous millennia of prehistory related by a novelist like Bruce, the current standard in archeology based on DNA analyses, as well as the more traditional dating of worked stone tools, accepts man into the new world around 11,000 years ago, give or take a millennium or two. Mainstream theories from only a decade ago, however, suggested there might have been a several migrations from Siberia starting as early as early as 42,000 years before the present age, an idea currently not in as much favor. Various migration dates seem to be proposed every few years, often based on state-of-the-art estimates of when glaciation lowered the water over the Siberian land bridge making such dispersals possible. When Bruce first told me about Calico, Louis Leakey was adamant that worked stone fragments there were evidence of human occupation at least 75,000 years ago. Some people now have gone so far as to state Calico offers up flakes from tools made 200,000 years before present.

I get the same reaction today from my archeologist friends that I got twenty-five years ago when I bring up Calico. They stuff their hands in their pockets, lower their gaze, shake their heads with that slightly embarrassed grin reserved for a layperson's question. No way, they say. The stones are in an alluvial fan deposited who knows when. It's a jumble, a mess, totally inconclusive. The stones were more likely flaked by natural geological processes than human hands. It's all just a remnant of the Leakey family ego, which drove them not only to discover some of the oldest hominids in Africa, but also to claim doing so in the New World. Even Mary Leakey didn't agree with her husband's assessment; and besides, the ancestors to *homo sapiens* hadn't even made it out of Africa and into Asia prior to a million years ago.

Of course, that was the opinion about the African migration last year. This fall strong evidence was published in support of our predecessors leaving Africa two million years ago, thus doubling the size of the window for speculation, not to mention my skepticism about the opinions of my expert friends. When I drove through here in September, on my move from Santa Fe to L.A., sweating buckets by 11 A.M. in the non–air-conditioned "blue turtle," as Beth called it, I pulled off to visit the Early Man Site. The road in was closed, but I locked up the Honda down by the gate to the landfill and walked up the stony drive. The only rock I picked up that day lay on the ground about two yards from the car and just outside the boundary of the site. A palm-sized piece of flaked stone, it looked to my untrained eye very much like what I would examine along the trails in New Mexico, where artifacts are literally so thick in some places you can't avoid stepping on them. I put the rock back down and walked on in.

I don't have enough geology to know what, if any, natural pressures are available to have produced the consistent layer of "worked" rocks I saw for the hour and a half I prowled carefully through the site, peering into deep trenches excavated in the alluvial layers at Calico. But I appreciate Bruce's insistence that we're not even close to understanding the memories of this region. Examination of the fossil record, DNA analysis, and digital side-scanning radar couldn't even accurately untangle the landfill next door, much less what might be a fire ring and associated garbage strewn about by someone between eleven and two hundred thousand years ago.

As I'm relaying all this to Beth we're passing "Lake Dolores" on the left (no water in sight, much less a lake) with its RV park and empty waterslide, and then a very crispy and unhappy-looking vineyard. On the right the Union Pacific tracks are being tended by a work crew with a vaguely prehistoric assemblage of cranes and winches. Just now, within a minute or two past Calico, the urban grid finally disappears on both land and map. The road ahead bears north by northeast, and aside from single- and two-passenger cars, usually a guy driving accompanied by a girl, the only other vehicles of note are charter buses bound for the casinos. I turn the page in the atlas to keep up with our position and prepare for the one side trip we've decided to take.

10:30 A.M. Ninety-five percent of the Mojave's 54,000 square miles is within three miles of some kind of road. Perhaps that's not surprising: It's the smallest of the country's five deserts (and trivial compared to the grandest of them all, the Sahara, at 3.3 million square miles); it's close to Los Angeles; and, Californians drive over 240 *billion* miles every year. Deserts as a class of geography are indicator regions of the planet, where even slight changes in the environment become visually evident almost immediately owing to lack of trees, a precarious ecosystem easily nudged out of balance, and little regular precipitation to wash away the evidence. Ruts from the Mojave Trail of the nineteenth century are still evident here, as are tank tracks from World War II training maneuvers. The Mojave is even more a portent of things to come because of its scale and proximity to a megalopolis, and roads are not just part of the picture, but our fundamental structuring of the landscape.

The notes in my lap remind me that 20 percent of the world's surface lies within its great desert systems, and that 25 percent of California is desert. At the end of this century about a sixth of the world's people now live within the deserts; some demographers predict that within a hundred years up to half of us may do so. The exurban growth of edge cities in the Mojave such as Victor-ville is a leading indicator of that trend. Becoming rapidly more than com-muter suburbs, they're forming a ring of linked communities that are mutu-ally self-supporting, where commuting occurs not into the city, into Los Angeles, but among themselves, from Barstow to Hesperia, from Twentynine Palms to Palm Springs. The roads spread throughout the world's deserts, out-ward from Cairo in Egypt and Riyadh in Saudi Arabia, as well as from Los Angeles.

All that stops the growth in the Mojave are the military bases—such as Fort Irwin just north of Barstow where maneuvers are still conducted 360 days a year in an area the size of Rhode Island—and those other strategic federal pre-serves, the wilderness and scenic areas, national parks and monuments. The grid dies down east of Calico because the available land is squeezed into a relatively tight corridor between Fort Irwin, the Mojave National Preserve, and a handful of wilderness areas.

Our short excursion this morning starts at mile 101.5, where we exit south onto Afton Road and head south on its dirt surface to intersect with the re-gion's oldest known road, the Mojave Trail, which became the Old Spanish Trail, the Mormon Trail, the Mojave Road, and is still the route of the Union Pacific Railroad whose tracks we followed up through Cajon Pass.

Afton Canyon is just outside the preserve and channels the mostly subter-ranean Mojave River until it dribbles out onto the flatland of Soda Dry Lake. The canyon is one of those few places where the river surfaces year-round, hence its popularity with early travelers, and the campground at its mouth is one we want to check out. We follow a wash down to the river with evidence of off-road vehicle use on every hillock around us. There's new barbed-wire fence strung on both sides of the road, an odd three-strand-barbs-one-smooth combination meant not to keep cattle off the road, but people on it. It doesn't rain often here, but when it does the erosion is fierce and tire tracks turn the natural process into a rout.

We bottom out, literally and figuratively, as we meet the bottom of the canyon, the campground to our left and train tracks going over the river to our right. Beth gets out first, scanning the sky to the west for the clouds we know are behind us; this wouldn't be a fun place to try and drive out of during a rainstorm. The sky's an overcast glare of pearl with nothing for us to worry about in the next hour. She wanders off to inspect the camping sites while I go over the road and under the railroad trestle to the river, which is marked by thick stands of that pernicious and thirsty invader, the salt cedar. There is, indeed, a slight flow of rancid liquid; maybe Francisco Garcés drank the water here in 1776, when he pushed through the trail to what would eventually be Los Angeles, but I wouldn't touch it today without a heavy-duty portable filter, iodine tablets, and maybe a few minutes of boiling just to make sure.

I'm quite satisfied, though, to be standing on the path that historically links Los Angeles to Las Vegas to Santa Fe. I note the blue and the red tags scrawled here, too, underneath the trestle, a sign of what might be called the New Spanish Trail, the path that attracts immigrant labor from L.A. to Las Vegas to work in the hotels and casinos. Thirty percent of all the jobs in the fastest growing city in America are in hotels, gaming, and recreation, though most of them are at the bottom of the pay scale. The advertisements placed by the personnel offices of the hotel-casinos tell how much you'll make an hour, and it sounds pretty good to someone just up from Mexico. But what they don't tell you is how expensive it is to live in Las Vegas. Rents there are cheap in comparison to elsewhere in America, but if you're starting at the bottom it means sleeping three shifts of people in a motel room or apartment, rotating bedtime in sync with the day, swing, and graveyard shifts at work. Six to twelve people per rental isn't uncommon. And the gangs follow along, parasites of the economic miracle of Las Vegas, where money and drugs mix well with ballistic urban growth and immigrant labor.

Between the off-road enthusiasts, who must roar through the canyon on weekends, and the less than genial spray-can devotees from East L.A., this is probably as uncomfortable a place as I can imagine staying. I meet Beth back at the car and she has the same impression, though the view into the canyon with its rising walls is temptation to return for a day hike.

This view is the first one where we can easily imagine ourselves into that faraway described by Bachelard, the canyon defining a space through which we can see ourselves walking and thus, to some degree, possessing. I don't mean "owning the land," but walking over ground to form a memory of it that we carry away, a tangible and retrievable experience that's more than just a picture. Driving gives us landscape memories, too, but they're usually much fainter mental traces, and the wider and faster the road, the more negligible the impression. The only escape from road amnesia is hooking the drive to another experience of importance—a vacation trip with your parents, the first excursion with a girlfriend—or, perhaps, counting overpasses and road kill for an essay. But even then, obviously, it's nowhere near as embedded in the circuitry as when you've involved your neuromotive self in the land. It's why I'll have to go back to Irving Street and walk the neighborhood if I want to get any closer to the memory of my great-grandmother.

The canyon also forms a room, a walled-in space set apart from the huge 360 degrees of the desert floor. Its steep and steadily climbing walls are bro-

Driving gives us landscape memories, too, but they're usually much fainter mer

ken by intimate side gullies and washes which quickly disappear from our view as they cut back deeply into the sediments of the canyon. They, too, form spaces we inhabit with our imaginations as we stand next to the railroad tracks with binoculars in hand. Like the multistoried castle walls it evokes, the very structure of the canyon invites us to compare our scale with its width and height. We pace it off in our minds and take up house, and we leave only with reluctance.

Driving back up the rutted wash, I can't help but compare Afton with that crenelated canyon defined by the Las Vegas Strip, the tall hotel-casinos of which also form a deliberate corridor in the desert. Thirty years ago the Strip was designed for driving at 35 mph, but when the buildings moved up to the sidewalks to extend the ambience of the casino outside, to push the floor shows onto the sidewalks, it became a walking experience. Now when you ask people to reminisce about a visit to Las Vegas, it's not what happened inside the casino that's first spoken about, but what's remembered of a walk through that playground canyon. By unconsciously aligning its urbanscape more closely to our experience of landscape, the city has made itself even more memorable. Las Vegas has constructed an urbanscape based on the landscape of expectation, as well as that unfulfilled desire to consume. The side gullies on Las Vegas Boulevard lead into hotel lobbies and our ability to inhabit the imaginary space is facilitated by what will soon total 120,000 rooms for rent.

11:09 A.M. Our detour takes us a total of only seven miles round trip and we're approaching the freeway sooner than we'd have liked; the only consolation is that we consider this an exploratory foray for overnight and day trips in the desert this winter. Just as we come off the dirt road at the overpass, a west-

ces, and the wider and faster the road, the more negligible the impression.

bound semi passes underneath pulling a twenty-four-foot cabin cruiser. Its white hull floats serenely above the road. Maybe they'll find the fabled Dolores Lake.

About seven minutes east we pass the third CHP officer of the day. He's pulled over a guy with two kids. Beth checks the speedometer and slows down. A few yards farther there's a sign advertising $1,000 fines for littering, under which starts a line of forty white plastic trash bags filled by the side of the road and awaiting pick up. Debris along this stretch of I-15 ranges from

3. Craig Stecyk, *Roadside Pour Shot, Casablanca, California,* 1985. Photograph © C. R. Stecyk.

quarter-mile-long zones of shredded truck tires to small pyramids of Styrofoam fast-food containers heaped up alongside fences, from the solitary but ever-present beer cans to entire mosaics of broken glass. In some places it looks as if everyone who's driven through the desert has thrown something out the window to memorialize their brief passage.

Craig Stecyk is a Los Angeles artist who's worked extensively with roads in the West. He once hypothesized, after driving the notoriously littered old Boulder Highway south of Las Vegas, that road glass forms alluvial deposits fanning out from the shoulder of the highway, its distribution determined by proximity to roadside bars; the closer you are to the bar, the thicker the glass. He actually proposed a gallery installation around the idea, where teenagers would have been hired to collect the glass and deposit it on the floor. Viewers were to walk over a footbridge to examine the collection and at the end of the exhibition the glass would be sold to a recycling center with the money used to pay the kids. That's about as good as an installation piece can get, a clever and, knowing Stecyk, probably handsome artwork built by kids who needed the work, and one which cleaned up a piece of the terrain while educating participants and viewers about both art and environment without preaching.

Stecyk also used to collect road kill on his driving trips, taking them back to his studio for bronzing. He disposed of the carcasses as they decomposed, but took the bronzes back to the original collection sites and bolted them down to the road. I don't know if that would have qualified him for a $1,000 ticket, but I'll bet the CHP behind us would have been unsure how to distinguish between memorialization and littering.

I finish writing down my Afton Canyon notes just as we come around Cave Mountain to our left, and put the binoculars in my lap in anticipation of what I predict will be the scenic climax of the trip. Past Rasor and Zzyzx roads, and then at mile 87.5 from Las Vegas, spreading south of us are Soda Dry Lake, Devil's Playground, and on the far side of a dark lava field the Kelso Dunes almost thirty-five miles away. Big dunes to which the eye is immediately drawn, skipping over the intervening territory; rosy golden six-hundred-foot-high dunes like something out of Arabia; a forty-five-mile-square patch of the Sahara at the foot of the Granite Mountains. Beth and I take turns steering for several miles as we cadge glimpses through the binos, a time-honored if not CHP-approved tradition for enjoying western scenery from a moving vehicle.

Even at such a distance from the road, the dunes help frame and make sense out of Las Vegas. There aren't, for instance, any sand dunes in that city, but there is the forty-four-year old Sands hotel-casino—or will be until 2 A.M. on November 26, my birthday, when it's scheduled to be imploded to make room for a new Venetian-themed 6,000-room resort. But the Sahara is also there and, before its demolition in 1994, so was the Dunes with its loosely Arabian sign. The Mojave isn't really a classic sandy desert like those of Africa and Saudi Arabia, but a stony one paved with volcanic debris and gravel. That's not, however, the point, lest we confuse fantasy with reality; the public identity of Las Vegas is primarily concerned with the former. Las Vegas continues to use our Hollywood image of the desert to great advantage, a place of eternal mystery where the rules break down, where heroic effort combined with chance can bring fame and fortune, or at least sultry women and darkly handsome strangers for a good time. The sight of the Kelso Dunes in the distance, as drivers race along the freeway from Los Angeles to the Nevada border, is reassuring. It means you're headed in the right direction, uncoupling yourself from civilization, throwing beer cans straight into the winds of freedom. You're living like Gary Cooper in the Foreign Legion, like Lawrence of Arabia, like the English Patient.

This dramatic tension is furthered by the presence of what is proclaimed to be the tallest thermometer in the world at Baker, a small strip of commerce that marks the road north to Death Valley and the last town before the Nevada border. Today the 130-foot-high thermometer reads 77 degrees. This vastly increases my respect for the credibility of this device, which bears more resemblance to a sign on the Strip than a scientific instrument: it's the first time

I've ever seen it read less than 96. In his thorough contemporary account of the region, *The Mojave,* David Darlington reports that he's never heard of it dipping below 120 degrees. Easily visible from the freeway, it's just as clearly an advertisement for the lure of the dangerous desert, the hazardous crossing we make until reaching the oasis of Las Vegas with its hundreds of thousands of palm trees, both the neon ones and those bought with wads of cash directly from the avenues and backyards of Los Angeles.

Even the road signs outside Baker conspire to dramatize the situation. The mileage sign states 89 miles to Las Vegas and 534 to Salt Lake City, the interval from sinner to saint apparently devoid of civilization in between. There's also a warning posted as we begin the long climb up to Halloran Summit: "Avoid Overheating: Turn off Air Conditioning Next 17 Miles." It's a sensible precaution, to be sure, but disconcerting after Baker's phallic thermometer.

11:45 A.M. We crest the summit, passing a semi grinding its way up in the truck lane with half a prefab home in tow. The driver has the window down, chin propped on his hand, shoulder jammed against the door frame. He doesn't look worried about anything, much less air conditioning. Across Shadow Valley and slightly north the 7,929-foot peak of Clark Mountain is drifting in cloud, while to the south the subtle 1,500-foot upswelling of Cima Dome rests in an uneasy play of sun and cumulus. Rain's on the way and as we coast downhill we pass three middle-aged guys in cowboy boots walking a gas can down to the valley. I keep an eye on the odometer and on the valley floor mark the Mobil station on Cima Road at about 3.3 miles. If they don't get a ride, they're looking at a six-and-half-mile hike, the return trip uphill and into the sun on most days. They're lucky it's cloudy and cool, even if they get wet.

Across the valley and up the other side is Mountain Pass, the third and final summit since Los Angeles, and now it's only 42.6 miles to where we'll turn into the outskirts of Las Vegas. On top at 4,730 feet, the view is classic basin and range, valleys running south to north in parallel with rank upon rank of peaks. It's raining to the south and east, and to the north in the Spring Mountains it's probably snowing up on Mt. Charleston, which stands over 11,900 feet. I hope the guys on foot in the valley behind us get a ride. Once again we're coasting downhill, Beth still striving to keep us under 80. We pass three more trucks pulling prefab halves, a sign of the more than decade-long housing boom in Las Vegas, where the city issued more building permits in 1995 than did Los Angeles.

The road turns sharply north in the Ivanpah Valley to run alongside the western edge of a dry lake bed. Ahead of us is a low saddle between this valley and the next, the Roach Dry Lake, that marks the state line and the end of San Bernardino County, though not quite yet the edge of my AAA map. We cross the saddle at 27.3 miles from town with Whiskey Pete's and the Prima Donna on the left and Buffalo Bill's on the right, three properties in what this month will officially become the town of Primm. These hotel-casinos are the beginning of frontier fantasy at its most contrarian, their combined 2,700 rooms and nearby eighteen-hole golf course plunked in the middle of what would be more appropriately the setting for a postapocalyptic disaster flick. Whiskey Pete's is, despite its name, eighteen stories dressed in a mock–Medieval castle façade, while across the way Buffalo Bill's is a like-sized mine-and-mill illusion completely surrounded by a red roller coaster, the tallest in the world.

Earlier this month Whiskey Pete's was the site of "Chance," a conference sponsored by the Art Center College of Design in Pasadena. Its featured speaker was the preeminent French philosopher Jean Baudrillard, who has proposed among other semiotic feats the demise of reality. The French are even better at hyperbole than Americans, often using linguistic exaggeration as a device to provoke debate over serious issues, most of which seem to involve the end of something, such as God or time. I wouldn't necessarily presume that's Baudrillard's tack, but only note it's a cultural characteristic and one totally appropriate to the hyperfantasy of Las Vegas and environs. Where more logical a place could there be to request a philosopher hold forth on the breakdown of reality than in a *faux* castle built next to a space-age freeway on the edge of an ancient alkaline dry lake bed at the end of the twentieth century?

Thirteen and a half miles down the road we approach another set of hotel-casinos flanking the road, Nevada Landing tarted up like a nineteenth-century Mississippi riverboat on the left and the Gold Strike, a false-front western town, on the right. The Nevada Welcome Center is located behind the latter and just west of the Sandy Valley Correction Center, which is just too good a juxtaposition to miss, so we pull in. The Welcome Center is a modest one-room affair, ferociously air-conditioned even on this rainy day. One wall displays direct phone lines to 82 of the 152 hotels shown on the map nearby, while another wall holds hundreds of racked brochures advertising helicopter flights over Hoover Dam and Lake Mead, hikes in the Red Rock Canyon National Conservation Area and Valley of Fire State Park, as well as rooms at each and every one of the hotels shown on that map across the room. In comparison with the state-line visitor centers in, say, Arizona, it's obvious that natural scenic beauty takes a backseat in Nevada as an attraction.

On our way out I pick up a thirty-two-page booklet called *Playing It Safe: A Player's Guide to Crime Prevention.* Inside, nineteen separate scenarios are listed to demonstrate how easy it is for a criminal to part you and your money: purse-snatching and mugging, holdups and con games. The only thing it doesn't warn about is losing money at the tables. Las Vegas is actually one of the safer resort cities in the world; the odds are minuscule that you'll be robbed while there. That's in direct contrast with the inevitable probability that you'll have the majority of your money taken away by the perfectly legal games of chance. Baudrillard has no irony more finely honed than that of the Welcome Center.

Once outside I briefly scan the correctional facility with the binoculars to analyze the fence, feeling almost as guilty as when counting tanks in Yermo.

Maybe it's barbed wire that induces the paranoia? This particular barrier is high and overtopped on the inside, but it's only a single fence with towers at the four corners, so it's not a high-security prison. Incarceration in the desert is a big business growing almost as fast as gaming. With more and more people being locked up—and Nevada has the highest per capita rate of incarceration in the nation—public officials run into the embracing question of where to house them. "Not in my backyard" is the oft-quoted response of neighbors to local prison construction, so once again the desert becomes a prime location for the storage of undesirable elements: radioactive isotopes, nerve gas, biological weapons, drug dealers, and purse snatchers. The possibility of escapees from any of those categories definitely increases the chance for excitement in the desert.

ONE

We're leaving the Welcome Center parking lot at 12:35 to drive the final eighteen miles to our turnoff. Beth catches herself doing 92 mph before slowing at our exit for Lake Mead Boulevard. She makes it with a foot or two to spare, the Honda's brakes proving conclusively their superiority over speed. We're going in the back door this time, still several miles short of the Strip and just skirting the event horizon of the city proper. We're actually in Henderson, a separately incorporated town that was created during World War II to manufacture gadgets out of the magnesium mined in huge quantities farther north. After the war the town specialized in producing rocket fuels, liquid chlorine, caustic soda, and other chemicals potent enough to cause what used to be referred to as "the Henderson cloud," an aerial gathering of powerful pollutants visible each morning from those Las Vegas hotel rooms facing south.

While there's still some industry in Henderson, the growth of Las Vegas has propelled land values way past rocket fuels and into the development of immense subdivisions. We pass a new one under construction, "Green Valley Ranch." Two hundred newly transplanted palm trees line its entrance, and they shift nervously in a light wind, the storm close on our heels. Some brown and yellow evergreens, hopelessly out of place, line a stucco wall surrounding the back walls of the first houses. A couple of miles down the street we come to another entrance for the same development, another two hundred palms lining the "Valle Verde" entrance. We can't decide if this means there's a bicultural division inside, Anglos to the west and Hispanics to the east. Or maybe the developers are trying, despite all obvious visual intelligence to the contrary, to make prospective buyers believe there's an authentic difference among their poured-out-of-the-can variations on red tile roofs and arched doorways because "Green Valley" has been translated into Spanish.

12:45 P.M. As we drive uphill on the southern rim of the valley, Sunrise Mountain to the east is fast losing what light it was able to collect during the morning. Thick dust blows under a canopy of black clouds, and the Strip is so murky that streetlights are coming on. The top of the Stratosphere Tower, at 135 stories the tallest structure west of the Mississippi, is as lost in the clouds as Mt. Charleston. It feels for all the world as if we did just "Enter the Night," though it's a more dystopian darkness than that promised by the billboard in Yermo. It's more as if we've been counting backwards to Ground Zero, which in reality for the last forty years has been stationed just on the other side of the mountains north of the city. You could lie on your back in a hotel swimming pool during the 1950s and watch the mushroom clouds, just another part of the burgeoning fantasy. Maybe this is what Baudrillard has in mind, that we've so thoroughly interwoven fact and fantasy together that, not only can we not distinguish the two from each other, but for all practical purposes they're the same. We've so altered our environment—the virtual space of our intellect as well as the external one—that even a relatively unchanged piece of terrain, like the Kelso Dunes, is simply subsumed by us to be part of the backdrop to our expectations. (That doesn't, however, mean we can't die of radiation or thirst in the desert; we can, should we step out of the vehicle of our fantasy, the car, and attempt to deal with reality on our own two feet for very long.)

Just as physical erosion both occurs and then becomes visible in the desert more quickly than elsewhere, and just as urban grid creep is vividly evident foot by foot without a screen of vegetation to disguise it, so the absurdity of our desires plays out more nakedly in Las Vegas than elsewhere. The desert offers the space and tenders us permission to take what in Los Angeles is a more personal and intimate expression of ego and desire, the house in all its costumes, and turn it into the most enormous theme park on the face of the planet. It's also a city that erodes as quickly as the desert. It's hard to reach the actual place we call Las Vegas because, as an exotic hybrid of Los Angeles, it's always trying to get there itself, always on the road and never arriving. The hyperactive landscape of Los Angeles—the earthquakes, floods, and mudslides—is nature's version of a teardown, where a perfectly good existing house is leveled in order to construct another. Homeowners like Aaron Spelling buy existing mansions in order, just naturally, to build even bigger ones. The landscape has set the rules of the house for Los Angeles, and that extreme tentacle of it, Las Vegas, exhibits the same behavior as the parent body, but exaggerated by the permission afforded by the desert. There's precious little stability in the physical infrastructure to which memory can attach itself.

Thirty million people visit Las Vegas every year, flying through the world's ninth busiest airport in a city with only 1.1 million residents (though with the number of people moving there annually quickly moving past the 75,000 level, they're now predicting two million by 2005). The oldest casino left in town, the El Cortez, an adobe structure built in only 1941, has now spawned eleven of the world's twelve largest hotels, one of which is the fourth largest pyramid in existence. Las Vegas has over forty *million* square feet of hotel rooms, and the length of stay has grown from 3.5 days in the early 1990s to a

It's hard to reach the actual place we call Las Vegas because .

solid four days per person as the fantasy grows more compelling to entire families.

For thirteen years during the 1980s and 1990s I spent an average of one week per month in Las Vegas on business for the Nevada State Council on the Arts. One of the gubernatorially appointed members of the council was the wife of a longtime casino owner who had an interest in the Union Plaza, the tall white hotel casino located at the western end of Fremont Street. Built over the site of the Union Pacific's railroad station, the building anchored one end of the original strip, Glitter Gulch. The staff of the council quickly figured out, once it was known we could afford to stay there courtesy of a prearranged state rate, that the best view from any hotel room in the city was from the seventh floor of the Union Plaza looking dead east over Fremont Street. The twin neon figures of Vegas Vic and Vicky lit up the street across from each other while below the hustlers and whores, pimps and cops mingled with the crowds. Pedestrians and cars jostled slowly for position as they cruised a street on which there was wattage enough to read a newspaper at midnight. The sun coming up over Sunrise Mountain shot straight down the street and into your room as if it were sweeping clean the town. That, however, was entirely too natural a scene for the younger set of casino owners.

First Steve Wynn, the man who brought us the Mirage with its volcano erupting on the Strip, tried to sell the city on canals for Fremont Street. I still find it hard to believe that he was unable to convert the city council to his vision, that they actually balked at using the water. (He's since taken his lust for aqua-fantasy back to the Strip, having just secured a billion dollar line of credit to build the water-themed Bellagio, which will feature a huge lake and aquatic show by the justly famous and supremely surreal Cirque du Soleil.) Instead, the property owners concocted "The Fremont Street Experience," a ninety-foot-high steel canopy covering the four blocks of the street leading up to the Union Plaza. Embedded in the flying arch are 2.1 million light bulbs which form the world's largest electronic readerboard, programmed to bring

always trying to get there itself, always on the road and never arriving.

us a variety of crowd-pleasing light shows. While walking the length of this amusement one morning with the local painter Robert Beckmann, I met the New York art dealer Ivan Karp.

Karp is the gallery owner who introduced America to Andy Warhol, the single contemporary artist who, for the most part quite deliberately, helped create our current version of pop culture in all its self-aware unreality. Karp is an art insider completely cognizant of where our culture has been, where it's going, and how it's going to get there. On his way that morning to the craps tables at the Horseshoe Club, Karp was dressed in black and wearing "a gambler's rosary," a sort of vernacular necklace featuring assorted miniature dice and a rare high-denomination poker chip. He thought the canopy was just one more outstanding example of Las Vegas going over the top. So to speak. I disagree.

Walking around Las Vegas with Robert Beckmann is always a revelation. The painter of more than two hundred murals in town since 1977, he estimates he's covered about 18,000 running feet with illusionary three-dimensional space on local walls, much of it in casinos and restaurants. He's created nineteenth-century train stations, desert dioramas, the backside of the moon, deep abstract geometries, and the inevitable Italian landscapes for pasta emporia. He supports his art, in other words, by creating the picturesque fantasies which are always in demand in Las Vegas. He's adept with the mathematics of architecture and illusion, the logic of visual space, and the placement of amenities. And he's as deeply frustrated by the Fremont Street Experience as I am.

We agreed it's clever in that its proportions mimic those of the aisles in the casinos bordering the street—or what used to be a street, but is now a sanitized pedestrian mall with all the liveliness of the New Jersey Boardwalk at three A.M. in February. The buildings are downscaled and trivialized by the ninety-foot loft of the canopy, and now look more like toy slot machines. Instead of the street functioning as a theater for the action of the crowds, it's become an unsuccessful parody of itself. There's no humor, no raunch, no sense that traffic is coming in from the desert filled with possibilities. Pedestrian flow is dispersed across the pavement instead of concentrated on the sidewalks, so it never reaches that ongoing critical mass of excitement routinely achieved in the past. Vegas Vick and Vicky are all but blocked by support columns. And the view from any floor at the Union Plaza down Fremont Street is gone, lost in structural steel.

The El Cortez has been moved at least twice to accommodate new construction; Robert's murals are perpetually being covered up or repainted as the casinos expand and reinvent their self-images. The Sands will be blown up on Tuesday, the Dunes was dynamited in October of 1994, the Landmark fell a year ago, and the Hacienda is scheduled to be imploded this coming New Year's Eve. Hollywood is always here in droves for the explosions, studio executives sipping champagne in suites carefully chosen for a safe view, film crews on the ground and in helicopters shooting footage that will be inserted into future action films. After all, why bother to build a cheesy set and blow it up when "real" shots are just down the road? The turnover rate in Las Vegas might be a little too high for a place I'd care to call home; but, given that, despite all best efforts to the contrary, the survival rate among artworks during a millennium might run as low or lower than 1 percent, who's to complain? If we didn't have the opportunity constantly to reinvent ourselves and civilization, society would be even more neurotic than it already is. And civilization here is definitely in tune with the erosive cycle of the land and its weather.

The difficulty is that the Fremont Street Experience is so earnest about its value as family entertainment, so deadpan in its virtue that it looks like a leftover piece of Main Street at Disneyland twenty years ago. Instead of glorifying the strength of Las Vegas, its good-humored venality, it attempts to capitalize on an alien wholesomeness, which can neither compete nor make sense. (Even Baudrillard was claiming to have taken $100 from the slot machines at Whiskey Pete's on his first night during the conference there. Presumably the money remained real.)

1:00 P.M. We're not stopping this time and cruise past first the exit for the Beckmann's house, and then Henderson's development frontier, where bulldozers have just bladed flat a raw pattern awaiting piles of lumber. A minute later, and at 282 miles from Los Angeles, we crest Railroad Pass; ahead and across the Colorado River a gray drape hides Arizona.

A week from now on the return trip we'll pull off to stay with Robert and his wife, Polly, who was his assistant on the murals for years before switching to the more predictable and welcome income of a schoolteacher. They're currently debating whether or not Robert should accept new mural commissions, or perhaps more accurately how many, a balance wavering between household budget needs and time available for Robert to pursue studio, which is to say noncommercial, art. While he's always working on his own canvases in bits and pieces, he painted his last major series in 1993, and he's gripped by that gnawing feeling familiar to every artist who accepts outside jobs for survival. There's not enough time for both his work and jobs, those two maddeningly related but widely different uses of the paintbrush.

So we'll sit on their back patio in the foothills of Henderson and discuss the offers while perusing with our binoculars the newly transplanted Manhattan skyline. This Christmas you'll be able to book a room in the Empire State Building—well, a slightly shorter version, to be sure—at the New York–New York hotel-casino. Come back next year for a room in Venice. From the Beckmanns' backyard, the bowl of the Las Vegas Valley is a coherent entity, the suburbs all blending together and forcing your vision ever down and inward to the Strip. Individual residential identity is given over to serving the greater good, the common fantasy that sustains the economy. It's an architectural scheme as clear and focused as the laser beam shot skyward from the apex of the Luxor's pyramid at night.

We can't remember ourselves easily in Los Angeles as a society, as a collective identity, because most of our architectural time and money has been residential. There are a few interesting corporate headquarters and some fine public buildings, to be sure, but the only cohesive civic architecture that's shared is the freeway—which is exactly the image most often conjured up in conversation with our friends who don't live there. That, and mansions belonging to the rich and famous. But neither can claim widespread recall in our cultural consciousness. Interstates 10, 5, and 15 are indistinguishable from each other. And no one besides a reporter for the *Los Angeles Times* can tell me offhand if Aaron Spelling's house is Tudor or Georgian, whether Geffen's estate is Casa California or neoclassical. Everyone, though, can identify signature properties on the Las Vegas Strip, their architectures designed to be advertised and to *be* an advertisement.

For now, though, we're on our way to Santa Fe, triangulating the only way we know how among the friends and memories of a life in the desert, by driving from place to place. It's an odd business, assembling points of memory into a personal map, the landmarks of which, the houses and casinos, are principally built on the shifting sands of fantasy.

The city slips out of the rearview mirror. I'm thinking of my mother and father who drove through the desert one spring night to write their own fable of independence and love. It worked for a while, perhaps for long enough. So may Las Vegas. So may Los Angeles.

Reno to Las Vegas

Drive Times

ONE

Stretching up my left arm as far as possible, on tiptoe with fingers extended to 7′7″ on the brick wall of the Riverside Hotel, I can just touch the top of the mud line that marks the high water of the flood. Behind me a thin stream of rancid liquid runs out of the shuttered building, into the gutter, down to the storm drain, and then into the Truckee River itself, which is twenty feet north and fifteen feet below me. There's a bathtub ring around downtown Reno this Valentine's Day, where six weeks ago the river overtopped its banks and closed the casinos on Virginia Street for the first time in their history.

At first they classified the flood as a hundred-year event, but it's the second time this has happened in forty years, so that doesn't seem right. Then they decided maybe fifty-year floods were much larger than originally determined by the U.S. Army Corps of Engineers. In either case there's a distinct lack of understanding in Reno about the relationship of the built environment to the natural. Across the river, skaters circle slowly to a Johnny Mathis tune from the early sixties', the outdoor rink surrounded by several dozen potted pine trees, a gesture that does nothing to disguise the flood damage nearby.

Walking over to where the water from the drowned Riverside dribbles out of the drain and into the river, I'm greeted by honks from three Canadian geese resting on a gravel bar below me. Normally I could descend to their level on the River Walk that parallels the water for a couple of blocks, but now it's cordoned off with yards of chain link fence. While most of the purple neo-Victorian attraction looks undamaged, its anchorage and electrical circuitry are obviously suspect. Completed in 1991 at a cost of $7.7 million, an unbelievably expensive amenity per linear foot, it's Reno's attempt to capitalize on an architectural history in which it participated only marginally, the mythical elegance of the dandified Old West. The Truckee is a vigorous mountain stream and an unwilling partner to urban civilization, a stubborn historical fact often ignored in favor of the fantasies that increasingly define the downtown.

I zigzag up Sierra, east on Court, and back to Virginia Street, cross the river and thus enter downtown proper, pad and pen in hand, a complete foil to the panhandlers who assume I'm a city official assessing flood damage. My first stop is the Woolworth's store, which opened in 1912 when Reno hosted more horses than cars. Sandbags block the front door. Though it's scheduled to reopen in June under its existing lease that runs until 2005, I think to myself: *Maybe.* I used to patronize the counter here during high school lunch breaks, but nowadays it's faster and cheaper for students to eat at Burger King and Taco Bell.

The elegant Art Deco façade of the Mapes Hotel across the way is also boarded up, but not from the flood. It's not economically feasible to bring it to life again as a hotel, the last of its furnishings were auctioned off in 1994, and most likely it will join the Riverside for demolition as part of the ongoing downtown "Renovation." The pattern in city planning here is to tear down the genuine historical structures and erect in their place postmodern simulacra of how we imagine the past, which are less expensive to build and easier to maintain. But the real shocker on Virginia Street is Harold's Club.

I'd heard it was closed, but the windows filmed over with the cataract of neglect are an unexpected and nasty sight. Holding up my pad to cut the glare, I peer inside and can't see any evidence of occupancy, not even a leftover strip of carpet. Like the Mapes, this is another cyclical disaster related to the ebb and flow of revenue and expenses. Harold's Club is one of the few properties downtown that never built a hotel, clinging to its status as a house of gambling, and not a gaming resort. While it allowed itself to partake in the traditional decor of the Wild West and hosted a gun museum, the club never took the big step into becoming a hotel-casino, and those that did—Harrah's, Fitzgeralds, the Eldorado—captured increasing numbers of the tourists.

Gambling is where patrons play cards and pull slot handles in smoky low-ceilinged rooms, where cocktail hostesses in low-cut blouses ply you with free drinks, and the pit bosses are ex-boxers. Gaming, its renovated version, takes place under the vaulted ceilings of theme environments, where your servers are dressed in period costumes and the pit bosses, men and women alike, resemble bank tellers. Gambling is best done at night when you're young and single, or old and single; gaming occurs when you're on family vacation and the kids are up on the mezzanine level in the video arcade, young gamers in training, as it were. And it's partly the difference between the two that's troubling downtown Reno.

I lower my pad and walk on, crossing the double set of railroad tracks which bisect the town. An average of fourteen trains cross town every day, some of them freights with a hundred cars, a mile-long vehicle taking up to fifteen minutes to pass in front of the idling traffic on every thoroughfare downtown. The recent merger of the Southern and Union Pacific railroads will increase that to at least as many as thirty-six per day, or one every forty minutes. Add in the transit time and you have gridlock every half-hour on the half-hour, twenty-four hours a day. Currently, the proponents of lowering the tracks seem to have the lead over those who favor construction of underpasses for the streets, a debate that's been going on since I was a kid. The flood would have wreaked havoc with either scheme. But the economic woes of the downtown coupled with the increased schedule seem to dictate solving the problem sooner rather than later this time around, and covering the track trench would have the additional benefit of adding five or six blocks of valuable real estate downtown. Fitzgeralds, on the south side of the tracks, isn't waiting around for the city council, and is planning to erect a 150-foot-long, $3 million skywalk over the tracks. Connecting with the Eldorado on the north side, it will then link Fitzgeralds into the extensive network of existing elevated crosswalks among the newer hotel-casinos on the north side of the tracks.

Once across the rails, I turn around to inspect the Reno Arch with its 800 feet of neon tubing and 1,600 light bulbs, a distant older cousin to the Fremont Experience in Las Vegas. Where it used to signify the entrance to the downtown, now it approximates the border between the southern downtown of the 1970s, the home of modern gambling in Nevada, and the newer northern section dominated by corporate gaming. For a while after this fifth version of the arch was built in 1987, the ubiquitous pigeons of Virginia Street shorted it out every night by flying inside and shitting on the circuits. The problem was solved with baffles, traps, and other aggressive deterrents, but that didn't stop local columnists from touting the pigeon poop as a condemnation of where Reno was headed.

Another block north is the Silver Legacy, Reno's newest and largest downtown property, a joint venture between the Eldorado and Circus Circus. When it opened in 1995 with its 1,700 rooms and 85,000 square feet of gaming, it was billed as the town's first Las Vegas—style resort. Part of the reason why is embodied inside the world's largest composite dome, a 180-foot-diameter white hemisphere looming over me as I cross Virginia Street to an entrance at one corner of the casino's block-long Victorian façade. Two interesting things have been built in Reno since I left in the fall of 1993, and inside the Silver Legacy is one of them. Not coincidentally, it's also a symbol of what's wrong with the downtown, and why the hotels have trapped themselves in the downward spiral of a cutthroat room-rate war as they compete against each other for customers, instead of against Las Vegas or other tourist destinations.

Swaggering past me as I go in is a tall guy in a tank top, jeans, and cowboy boots, who drops his Coors Light on the sidewalk where it empties out a stream of warm beer on the fake cobblestones. His girlfriend, dressed in black jeans and three-inch heels, punches him in the tattoo for littering. He laughs, putting his arm around her and throwing back his shag of dirty blond hair. I push open the second set of double doors and enter the loudest casino on the face of the planet.

This isn't anything I've measured scientifically, but instantly intuit, knowing that no human alive could bear a single added decibel and still function, much less drink and gamble, no matter how much pure oxygen they pump into the casino to keep us awake. Several hundred slot machines are whirring, buzzing, clacking, and clanging. Alanis Morissette is screaming about postcoital depression over the public address system, interrupted every thirty seconds by the operator paging various customers to call her. The operator, not Alanis, or so I think. The pianist in the bar underneath the four massive legs of the Mining Machine, a towering attraction of girders and fake nineteenth-century industrial machinery housed under the Silver Legacy's dome, is doing a full-bore honkytonk number. I sidle past him to the escalator, in retreat before an employee bustling up to me in a pink Victorian dress and a gray wig. She's—at least I assume it's a woman—handing out coupons for the buffet upstairs. . . . But what I'm here to check out is the 120-foot-tall geegaw above me that fills the interior of the dome, which is currently lit to resemble a night sky.

The escalator spews me out into the arms of a five-member Chinese ensemble playing traditional folk tunes, as behind me the pianist is joined by a banjo player who begins to pick out a loud version of "Yankee Doodle Dandy." I was wrong about adding extra decibels; it *is* possible. Next to me the Mining Machine, a hybrid fantasy of a stamp mill—assay office—mineshaft headframe, lets out a long whistle as its enormous gears, belts, conveyors, and cranes rattle up to speed. Dozens of red and gold lanterns are hung here and there from the structure in celebration of the Chinese New Year, as well as a gaudy dragon climbing the northwest girder-and-truss assembly.

Two guys in black are hanging from ropes and fussing with bolts, but I can't tell if they're part of the show or actual workmen, and that's exactly the problem with the Silver Legacy, downtown Reno, and anywhere else in the world that seeks to emulate Las Vegas. I'm scribbling and flipping pages on my pad, circling the tower as I write, and have picked up a short barrel-chested se-

4. Jeff Brouws, *The Mining Machine at the Silver Legacy, Reno, Nevada.*
Photograph © 1997 by Jeff Brouws.

curity guard who is discretely tagging me from about five yards back. We continue the circuit together. In front of me a portly woman in turquoise polyester pants is asking her husband: *What's it do, Charlie? Do you think we can go up in it?* Charlie mulls this over for a minute, video camera held in ready position at his right shoulder. *No*, he says, *I think it's just for show.*

The dome above us begins a slow fade into orange as dawn breaks over the tower and birds start chirping, amazingly audible over the Chinese band to whom I've now returned. There's no way for customers at the Silver Legacy to interact with this thing, and that's why it's a failure. I don't know how many cubic feet it takes up, and how many potential slot machines it displaces, but it's probably more expensive than the city's River Walk in terms of combined construction cost and lost annual revenues. That's quite a sacrifice for a large but ultimately trivial amusement, and the management has been asking local residents to suggest how they might improve it. Ideas range from gunfighters chasing each other from level to level, tours for the public, and nude dancers gyrating in cages. Despite the aesthetic diversity, all the proposals have one thing in common: people in the structure. That's what Hollywood has led us to expect from our fantasies at the end of the second millennium; that's why Las Vegas is successful, and why it's almost impossible to envision any other city catching up. Only Las Vegas can afford to match our expectations.

I stop to enumerate this on my pad, the security guy likewise pausing, ostensibly to admire some fancy fingering by the banjo player below us. I wonder if he's as dizzy from our third circuit around the tower as I am. Here are the rules governing architectural fantasy as I understand them:

First, pick an exotic place and/or time that a broad audience has been preconditioned to consider desirable by the movies and television. It can't be too exotic, nothing educational and high-brow like the Galapagos of public television, but more middlebrow fare, for instance, Bali (*"The Road to Bali"* with Bing Crosby and Bob Hope), the Old West (*"Gunsmoke"* and *"Bonanza"*), or Rio de Janeiro (Crosby and Hope again).

Second, design the environment not to represent the actual place, but our mediated image of it. If it's the South Seas, create a mock rain forest, stock it with animatronic parrots, and design swizzle sticks to match. If it's the Old West, use a typeface on the slot machines to mimic wanted posters from the era of Wyatt Earp. Color-coordinate the carpets with reinforcing motifs and hire muralists to decorate the walls with stereotypical images. Seventy percent of our sensory input is visual, 80 percent of everything we learn comes through our eyes. Hollywood has made trillions of dollars based on those percentages.

Third, involve your customers in the fantasy. At New York–New York (the Las Vegas version) you can ride a roller coaster and buy a hot dog at Nathan's. At the Paradise, a Circus Circus project in Las Vegas which will replace the demolished Hacienda, they're planning a surfing beach with six-foot waves, a reef where you can snorkel with tropical fish, and a shark exhibit where you can swim up to the man-eaters separated by only a pane of glass.

Fourth and final, don't ever look back. In terms of popular entertainment, we're conditioned to move into more and more elaborate and compelling virtual fantasies, whether it's through action movies with increasingly expensive special effects, video games where we insert our entire bodies into the action, or CD-ROM games where we determine the script as we play.

Las Vegas is the main drag of the American imaginatic

The Silver Legacy started out with what may have been a valid premise. Being a joint venture of the Eldorado and Circus Circus, the owners had experience in Las Vegas and knew the rules. But what was planned as an inventive new theme for a casino, a sixteenth-century Spanish seaport with galleon rides, turned into a half-hearted Victorian painted lady with a glorified erector set as an elaborate folly, a retread of the Old West theme pioneered by Las Vegas as early as the 1940s. The downtown properties are chewing on each others' room rates because this is the best they can do; they can't begin to compete for the Las Vegas customer in this arena. All that Reno can muster is a giant toy model, versus Las Vegas, which is busy perfecting architecture as mass entertainment.

Las Vegas is the main drag of the American imagination and Reno just an alleyway; there's not enough money available to change that, hence the dangerous downsizing of the Silver Legacy's ambitions. In order to stay on the cutting edge of the fantasy machine, you can't just be profitable but have to rake in sinful amounts of money, which Las Vegas has been able to do, despite the fact that Reno had casinos first. For one thing, the Truckee Meadows can't hold all the infrastructure to run enough large casinos to attract the massive number of customers upon which to project sufficient revenues to raise the billions in capital to build mega-casinos with enough cash flow to afford the fantasies. It's the closed loop of a Catch–22.

At this point I give up trying to write. Overhead a thunderstorm proceeds to boom its way across the dome, complete with strobe flashes. Even the security guy cranes his neck for a look at the cumulus projected from the light booth. Tucking my pad beneath my arm I bounce down the escalator to a cheerful melody from the piano bar and head for a door. On the way out I notice that debit card machines have been affixed to the inside rails of the 21

d Reno just an alleyway.

tables, a much more efficient way to separate a customer from a bank account than when I counted coinage in my twenties at Harold's Club. At least they got that part of the technology right.

Outside, the sun is about halfway down, reminding me that, despite the traditional lack of windows and clocks inside a casino, time does still exist on a track independent of blue and orange gels, preprogrammed light shows, and taped thunder. It's time for a coffee break, which I hope will reset my internal clock. I decide to have coffee at my favorite caffeine den, *Deux Gros*

Nez, a small upstairs hangout close to the Nevada Museum of Art that was started by a bicycle racer and his friends. It features signed racing jerseys, old bicycles, and more visual clutter per square foot than a casino. But it all hangs together in a narrative that's locally embedded, which leads me to consideration of the second interesting recent construction in town, a truck stop.

TWO

"The Biggest Little City in the World" started out as a river crossing in 1857 for emigrants and goods to California, first with a modest log bridge, then in 1861 a toll bridge and inn, and soon thereafter the progressively more substantial structures needed to bear up under the weight of the silver transported from Virginia City to San Francisco, a flow of wealth that virtually built Baghdad-by-the-Bay. By the time the extraction of minerals went bust at the end of the century, Reno had a solid enough footing as a banking and mercantile center that it could survive. The neighboring railroad town of Sparks shuttled trains in its massive yards, and industries located here to take advantage of Nevada's favorable tax climate, including a business concern of my Great-grandfather Lyman, Boss Manufacturing, which was then the largest producer of cotton gloves in the world.

The point is that, although Bill Harrah and Pappy Smith arrived in the 1930s, eventually turning what were glorified bingo parlors into the state's first full-service casinos, respectively Harrah's and Harold's Club, Reno has had a longer history as a transportation hub than a gambling center. It's often said that Las Vegas wouldn't exist as it does today if Reno hadn't broken ground first, but the oldest known pair of dice in the state are 2,300-year-old bones, and card games were a staple of the nineteenth-century mining camps. Reno had its heyday as a divorce capital in mid-century; by the 1970s Reno was already suffering a painful comparison to Las Vegas, which was just beginning to engage the massive warp engines of capital inflow. The reclusive industrialist Howard Hughes had bought up five casinos down south and Harold's Club up north. He transformed what had evolved over three decades as family-owned businesses into respectable corporate entities carefully engineered to mine individual greed cost effectively, a new kind of extractive industry. Once his managers documented that the ever-increasing flow of casino money could be kept relatively clean, the contest was over. What Las Vegas had built was at first financed by crime syndicates from back East, then a Mormon-run local bank; now it would be underwritten by Wall Street.

Despite the natural beauty of its setting between the northern Sierra and the desert, and its proximity to Lake Tahoe and world-class skiing, not to mention Virginia City, the largest historical district in America and an actual piece of the Old West, Reno made a series of marketing errors stemming in no small part from the collective ego of the downtown property owners. Instead of capitalizing on those existing attributes, it decided to imitate Las Vegas. Instead of a Hard Rock Cafe downtown, it ended up with Dick Clark's Bandstand, a juke joint selling t-shirts that rents a corner of the defunct Harold's Club.

There's also the suspicion that perhaps America can only market such dense fantasies regionally, and that Las Vegas pretty much has the West sewn up. Instead of the Japanese businessmen who visit Caesar's and drop six figures at the baccarat table, the Silver Legacy attracts the guy in the tank top discarding his Coors on the sidewalk. Reno keeps building more hotel rooms, which leads to price wars, which in turn attract less affluent customers. This self-defeating spiral drives down not only the take per person, but overall gaming revenues. It's a good formula for civic bankruptcy, decreasing your revenues while increasing your associated expenses, such as utilities and social services for the chronically underpaid service people and their families.

Finished with my coffee, I go to look at the truck stop, a ubiquitous form of functional architecture found along the interstate freeway system, their tall metal awnings stretched over semi-trailer trucks gulping up hundreds of gallons of diesel. The one that interests me sells no fuel and is located not next

to a freeway, but high up on a hill in southwest Reno, and houses the art
dealer Peter Stremmel, his wife, daughter, one of the best contemporary art
collections in the state, and a room full of finches.

THREE

As I drive south through town, past Virginia Lake swarming with ducks, coots,
cormorants, and three varieties of geese, I think about how Peter and his wife
Turkey Stremmel, a noted art restorer, could build such a house. Peter owns
the most successful art gallery in the state. He not only handles most of the
contemporary artists of note in the Great Basin, but also turns over the occasional nineteenth-century Remington or Farny, and maintains a long-standing
partnership with the blue-chip New York dealership Acquavella, selling early
twentieth-century European masterworks to the Japanese. (Nevada in general,
and Reno in particular, maintain a favorable tax status for the warehousing of
goods, whether it's cotton gloves by Lyman or oils by Rouault.)

The first house the Stremmels built in southwest Reno was a Santa Fe–
style hacienda. Comfortable, unobtrusive, and well suited to their needs at
first, it nonetheless was imitating a mongrelized style that had originated
elsewhere and been imported to Reno as a minor variation on domestic fantasy. As their taste in art grew increasingly contemporary, the Stremmels' desire to adopt a vocabulary that matched their changing aesthetics became
more and more pressing. As a result, they commissioned the boldest residence in the state, which just now comes into view. It's a move that has long-
term significance to the future of Reno in its relationship to Las Vegas, if anyone will pay attention.

The house, designed by Austrian-born Mark Mack, sits above town on one
of those hills to which I'd ride my bike as a kid, a typical stoop-shouldered
Great Basin mound of dirt and shattered rock held together by sagebrush.
Much of Reno is visible to the east and north, while to the south the Sierra

5. Jeff Brouws, *The Stremmel House, Reno, Nevada*. Photograph © 1997 by Jeff Brouws.

rises up to the 10,776-foot summit of Mt. Rose. Below and to the east of the house are the white fences and green fields of a once-rural residential area, and then the first of the desert mountain ranges. Against this lovely, arid, and muted palette Mack has designed, basically, a truck stop.

Well, it's a little more complicated than that. But the twenty-six-foot-high galvanized steel shed under which sit three colorful blocks was inspired by a drive Mack took on Interstate 80 east of town. At night, driving across the Great Basin, the brightly lit truck stop is a classic sight, often visible from thirty or forty miles away across the desert floor. It can take half an hour to reach the lights, even at freeway speeds, where the semis idle beneath the immense awnings of auto-industrial America. It's not cowboys and Indians, but nonetheless an authentic western image, and the architect has correctly pegged it as a valid source of architectural vocabulary pertinent to Reno's history as a crucial transportation node.

Mack has taken the primary colors of the trucks (don't we always associate red with the trucks of his namesake bulldog company?) and transmuted them into the appropriate tones: the dusky yellow of chamisa in bloom, sage green, the purple of a nearby lichen. It's a surprising, even off-putting house when first seen; it takes getting used to, but only improves with acquaintance. Like all good stories, it can be read more than once and still reveal new aspects of itself. Acknowledging our artifactual presence in the desert by quoting a truck stop, it's also sensitive to local conditions. The colors of the three primary blocks of the house appear almost too bold at first, until you realize that they, too, are a quotation, this time of the colors existing on the very ground around the house. This upsets our stereotype of the desert as brown dirt. The house makes us pay attention to and think about where we walk, the oldest use for stories that we have as a species. The Apaches say "wisdom sits in places," and architecture has as much ability to evoke place instead of destroy it, to slow us down for a story instead of speeding us up into the race of hyperconsumerism typified by corporate gaming.

The idea here is that Reno could develop a set of stylistic architectural conventions based on its own reality and history. It wouldn't be imitation anything, but could become itself. Instead, the most recently announced downtown project is another mega-hotel-casino planned to take up two city blocks with 2,000 rooms. The theme? a tropical island. The attractions? a luau buffet, an indoor pool with live palm trees, and a showroom. It's the Tropicana in Las Vegas circa 1958 all over again.

It's important to examine Reno as a place because it suffers from what other cities in America may fall increasingly prey to, the temptation to emulate Las Vegas. I don't mean simply copying its look, the riverboat casinos in New Orleans notwithstanding (which, of course, Las Vegas borrowed from the Mississippi in the first place), but the desire to theme the core of a downtown around some ideal location that has no local rationale, as if Disneyland's Main Street should exist everywhere from Seattle to Bangor. Maybe it's because I'm living in L.A., literally between Disneyland and the Universal City Walk, the two most visited attractions in the city, the latter a *faux* Los Angeles–in–Los Angeles to which one pays a price to be admitted. Could be I'm getting sensitive, but I see signs of theming from Florida to North Dakota. Taking the River Walk as a small example, theming is expensive and prone to being undermined over time by local conditions.

It's not that the downtown property owners should imitate Stremmel, anymore than they should copy Las Vegas, but that they should allow themselves to risk being creative, to gamble, in short, taking on the commitment they ask of their customers. While they might lose a property here and there in the process, all of downtown is just going to sink slowly otherwise. In exercising originality they would stand to become a viable alternative to Las Vegas, allowing them to compete in a much larger economic arena.

I head back on Lakeside Drive to visit the geese one more time, whom I sorely miss in Los Angeles. It's now late afternoon and they've flown over by the hundreds from the lake to the Washoe County Golf Course where they're grazing on the fairways, much to the consternation of a foursome about to tee off. The reason Reno's golf courses have been invaded by so many geese is that the Stillwater Marshes, about sixty miles east of here and a major stopping place on the Pacific Flyway for waterfowl, are drying up during most years, in large part because of the increasing amounts of water Reno diverts from various sources for both residential growth and downtown expansion, not to mention thirsty fairways built in what is most definitely a desert. The golfers and the geese are in this together, and I'm glad to see that, at least in this instance, they appear to be tolerating each other.

FOUR

Saturday, February 15: Triangulation

Now that I've spent yesterday single-handedly solving Reno's intractable economic woes, which to date have defeated the entire local business community and a decade of hired consultants, I can concentrate today on how all this relates to driving and memory, to land and landscape.

As Beth and I drove into Reno yesterday on US Highway 395 through Washoe Valley, I reminded myself that freeways aren't only designed to keep our attention away from the landscape, they're actually antistory. They're factual architecture at an extreme of functional focus, a perfect mid-ground, making it difficult for you to look at figures in the foreground—you're not supposed to be examining the expression on the face of the guy next to you while cruising at 75 mph. Nor are you supposed to let your gaze wander too far into the background, the landscape. Eyes on the road, please, a command from the Department of Motor Vehicles instruction manual that I was doing my best to ignore as I drove from Santa Fe to Las Vegas over two years ago. Nature, however, also has something to say about this, and in the winter of 1997 the landscape around Reno came close to swallowing the roads.

Washoe Lake has its ups and downs; at its deepest in wet years around eighteen feet, it's just shallow enough to catch the mast of your capsized catamaran. Flipped upside down on one of the frequently windy summer afternoons, you can't right your boat without leverage provided by helpful witnesses, one of the more embarrassing and well-deserved comeuppances for sailing in a desert lake. In really dry years the lake reverts to a dusty playa, thousands of two-foot-long catfish skeletons rattling around in the dust, which was the state of Washoe Lake in 1939 and again in 1994. This year, however, after three unprecedented back-to-back years of record snowfall and melt in the Sierra, the lake rose over the road in January and closed it, and was still lapping literally within inches of the pavement as we drove by. A "story" has been intruding on the road as the background, the landscape, rises to disrupt the traffic.

My memories also have something to say about the nature of this road, even though interstates are so generic as to almost defy the formulation of memory. I pointed out to Beth where the Washoe Pines divorce ranch, now an environmental center, is nestled up among the ponderosas on the west side, the Sierra side, of the valley. The hills where I rode up to Little Valley are still recovering from a forest fire that kept me from getting to work several years ago. I don't need a map and ruler to make the triangulations here.

One of my great-granduncles, the older brother of my great-grandfather over on Irving Street in L.A., was Dean Briggs Lyman. A mining engineer, he worked in Virginia City during the heyday of the Comstock Lode, but took time off in 1865 to get married by riding horseback down the hill to Washoe City, then the nearest county seat. Washoe City was a booming mill town halfway between Reno and Carson City that provided lumber for the mines, but eventually Reno's population and political clout grew enough to capture the county government, and the town has long since vanished. While my mom and I sat out her Nevada residency requirement for the divorce in 1959, I'd ride my favorite sorrel from Washoe Pines over to the remains of the townsite. Many ruins then populated Washoe Valley, the low-lying trough between Reno and Carson City, including what was supposed to be a Pony Express station, a stamp mill where ore from the mines was crushed, a narrow gauge railroad track, and more.

The mining engineer's son, George Lyman, was born in Virginia City in December of 1882, and eventually ended up as a doctor and chief of pediatrics at a hospital in San Francisco. His passion, though, was collecting books on California and Nevada, and he was thought in the 1930s to have the largest private collection of such in existence. The attraction was apparently a compelling one; Lyman himself would go on to publish several books with Scribners about the history of the region, in particular the role Comstock silver played in financing the infill of the San Francisco Bay in order to create some of the ground upon which the city was constructed, as ironic a transfer of real estate values as I can imagine. At this point I'm not only triangulating geography out of family history, but excavating the lineage of this essay as I write it. It's not just my thirty-three years of residency in Reno that provide the requisite memory to convert location into place for me here, but literary heritage. I'm proud of having another writer as a predecessor, yet sometimes as shy about that fact as standing around a military installation. It feels to me like a loaded fact I may have to live up to someday.

In fact, the entire drive up to Reno from L.A. was an unbroken reading of the road as narrative, which I could relate outloud to Beth who had never seen before the sweep of the eastern Sierra. I've accumulated many of my one million-plus road miles in the fifteen cars I've driven up and down US 395 since 1967, and every mile seems to have a campsite connected to it, a climb, a favorite place to eat, or even just memories of specific storms. And each of the stories has a moral or an instructive point, sometimes one that was apparent immediately, but more often one that took awhile to develop, perhaps rising into consciousness when passing through a particular place the next time around.

Overall, the lesson I've gained is to pay attention for I will not come this way again. Every passage through the land rewrites the landscape, whether it's literally through the slow accumulation of pollution or the wear and tear on the road, or metaphorically as memories are altered with the intake of new information about a place. No place ever looks the same twice, not only because it's changed perceptibly by our passage, but because reality is asymptotic, which is to say we constantly approach it, but never quite reach whatever "it" is. We're perceptual creatures, a work-in-process. Triangulation, as I've been using the word, is a way of approximating one's position, of momentarily fixing it, in both time and space. Tomorrow we'll make the third and last drive into Las Vegas—though every drive to Las Vegas is always the last one. Not only is Las Vegas never the same from visit to visit because of our mutating perceptions, but also because it revises itself so ruthlessly over very short periods of time.

In honor of the triadic nature of the work, we'll also add a third person to the journey. David Abel is a poet, editor, bookdealer, and jack-of-all-literature from Albuquerque, a vertical integration of the book industry within a single six-foot-one-inch frame, complete with wild black hair, glasses sliding perpetually down his nose, and the ability to be late for almost any occasion. His mania for counting is so extreme that he's known for writing and performing successfully to the second a poem about what can happen within two minutes and meant to be read in exactly two minutes.

He is, needless to say, perfect for this kind of thing, able to discourse upon Proust, analyze the typographical nature of highway signs, and to turn effortlessly the counting of semi-trailer trucks into metaphor. He's grabbed the opportunity to accompany us on this trip, using as his excuse to come to Reno the chance to sell rare artists' books to the University of Nevada Special Collections—and to play some poker, a method of counting with which he regularly supplements his income. We'll have three vantage points from within the car, three closely related but distinctly different points of view during the drive, yet another subset of triangulation.

FIVE

Sunday, February 16, 7:46: Sparks

I'm beginning to regret that I've chosen to wear shorts for the drive, Reno in February not generally encouraging that kind of behavior, this morning being no exception. I'm counting on the temperature warming up as we go south, hitting the mid-70s when we reach Las Vegas. Not willing to gamble with their comfort, Beth has on her pile climbing jacket and David is bundled up in the coat he wore to drive cabs in New York City several lives ago. As our first point of interest for the day, I've chosen Sierra Sid's Union 76 Truck Stop in Sparks, the last fueling point directly off Interstate 80 as it heads east into the desert. And I'm standing outside the car pumping gas while Beth plays quarter slots inside and David counts trucks.

Despite my choice of attire, which is attracting bemused attention from a trucker as he heads into the casino—and who is he to stare, I want to know, wearing nothing on top but a black t-shirt? Anyway, despite my cold knees, it makes sense to start here, given the Stremmel house. The contrasts and similarities are instructive. Starting with what's similar, there's a high awning engineered to withstand the 100-mile-an-hour winds that are frequent here in spring, and three trucks of varying colors idle underneath it, taking up only part of the space meant to accommodate up to sixteen rigs at a time.

The interesting difference is the westernized trim added around the rim of the awning, replete with several hundred outdoor light bulbs, in order to tie it in with the architecture—or, more correctly, the decorations on the casino—that signify there's gaming connected to the diesel. There's no art here to speak of, only construction with trim and a sign, which Venturi identified as the original commercial architecture of the Strip, the "decorated shed." It's road architecture, virtually as functional as the road itself, telling no story and needing the trim and signage even to identify it.

Beth returns first, having lost the four quarters I'd scrounged from inside the Honda, plus three dollars of her own. *I was up twelve credits,* she says, shaking her head, *but kept playing. . . .* Now David is back. He's counted only seventy semis, eight of which are cabs only and five nonsemis, plus ten trailers without cabs, and he's disappointed. *Good counting,* I reply. Beth tells him her tale of woe, and he blinks rapidly in response.

But that's what I did last night at the Peppermill! he exclaims. And I know better!

Pulling up the on ramp, I grin at David's wounded professionalism. Experienced pokerhead or novitiate slot puller, the temptation is the same. Even working at Harold's Club and knowing the odds on individual games, I'd still ritually throw away twenty or so bucks a month on 21 or slots. It's not that you think you can beat the odds, just that addiction to the cyclical struggle with the odds and the inevitable disappointment.

It's 8:09 and we're on the road, passing the abandoned Helms gravel pit on the left. It's now contaminated with oil leaking from the nearby petroleum tank farm; the City of Sparks plans to turn it into a lake for its park system. They've been pumping out and treating six million gallons a day, and studying how to stabilize its steep slopes, but the floods have altered the timetable a bit. Seems as if 900 million gallons of water poured in during the flood, raising the level of water in the pit by sixty-five feet in thirty-six hours, a process that the state's environmental officials thought previously would take three years. The high water eroded the banks of the pit almost up to the freeway, causing about two inches of subsidence in the roadbed of the westbound lanes, and there's much head scratching over who's to pay to empty the pit so they can continue to stabilize it.

8:10 A.M.: Truckee River Canyon A minute later we enter the twenty-five-mile stretch of I-80 that was the most expensive to build as it crossed the state. Typical of many transportation corridors in the West, where there are only a few optimal passages through the landscape, it's been used by emigrants since the mid-1800s and carries traces of prehistoric trails, old roads, the railroad tracks, power and telephone lines, and anything else that needs to go from east to west through this part of the Great Basin. What took three days to traverse a hundred years ago takes less than twenty minutes today. This canyon was my first experience driving out of town when I was fifteen and working on a learner's permit in a VW bug, a car in which I was forbidden to leave the city limits. Not much has changed except my attitude; primal fear of the open road where prehistoric semis roared by has been replaced with cruise control.

Lockwood, a settlement just inside the mouth of the canyon, has grown from a few ranch houses into a subdivision of immobilized mobile homes, many of which are regularly threatened by floods in a normal year, much less this one. If they'd just left them mobile, I can't help but think. The Mustang Ranch, one exit further and maybe the most famous whorehouse in America, still sits behind the huge auto wrecking yard. I've always been attracted more to the junk in the yard as art supplies than to the whorehouse, which indicates how my priorities developed as a teenager. Tracy Station Power Plant, letting off its white plumes of steam in the brisk morning air, still hosts mallards in its cooling ponds. My first exposure to the industrial sublime, albeit at a much smaller scale than either Hoover Dam or the power plant outside of

Not much has changed except my attitude; primal fear of the open roa

Holbrook, it's still a sight I look forward to when entering the canyon. Just beyond is the diatomaceous-earth processing plant, which turns everything around it in summer as white as if it were a winter snow. Accumulated over millions of years on the floors of ancient seabeds, the white vein is mined above us to our right, but is visible across the canyon, as well. The silica shells of the single-celled diatoms are used in swimming pool filters, another curious transference of real estate, this time from the Nevada desert to the wilds of Beverly Hills.

8:28 A.M.: Derby Dam Traffic seems relatively light for Presidents' Day Weekend, maybe six vehicles in sight at any given moment, and trucks are running
about one in four as we take Exit 36 to Derby Dam. This is a place I missed entirely as a kid, but it's the most important modern site in the canyon. Here, in
1905, is where the first dam was built by the U.S. Bureau of Reclamation.
Billed as a way to make the desert bloom, to recover a useless wasteland and
turn it into productive farmland, it was the forerunner of all the big water
projects in the West, from the Hoover and Grand Coulee dams to the California Aqueduct that diverts the water all along US 395 in the Owens Valley and
sends it to my tap in Los Angeles. Driving three days ago from L.A. and past
Mono Lake, Beth and I paralleled most of that water's path. This morning
we'll follow the water that originates in the Sierra around Lake Tahoe as it
passes through Reno, and is then diverted here, at the dam, to flow eventually
through Fallon and on to Stillwater, where it ends, as does all water in the
Great Basin, in a natural sink.

   The exit road is paved for a few hundred yards, then turns to dirt where it
passes underneath the railroad tracks. On the other side of the embankment
it's clear that the river has been up here, too. The road is a churned mess, mud
is still plastered just beneath the ties, and debris is hung everywhere through-

where prehistoric semis roared by has been replaced with cruise control.

out the brush. We park and clamber out, the temperature already ten degrees
warmer than when we left this morning.

   There's not much drama to see: a quiet bend in the Truckee, tall golden
reeds, a small V of geese flying west into Reno. But right here is the starting
point for decades of the most contentious water battles in America. The
Derby Dam diversion takes water out of the Truckee, which is already dimin-
ished in both quantity and quality by Reno upstream, and thus lowers Pyramid Lake at the terminus of the river. That makes spawning for various fishes,

upon which the native Paiute depend as a food source, extremely difficult. The diverted portion of the river, channeled through the Newlands Ditch, flows into and out of Lahontan Reservoir, through the agricultural communities of Fernley and then Fallon, and leaches natural toxic chemicals from the soil in addition to the manmade ones from fertilizers, which are then carried to Stillwater where they cause massive die-offs of fish and waterfowl. Further, Fallon wouldn't even exist without the diversion in the first place, and now that various legal settlements with the upstream urban users, the Indians, and the environmentalists have been hashed out in Congress and the courts, the farmers are losing water rights to both Pyramid and Stillwater.

The history of water in the West is replete with anomalies, but here's one that pivots around where Beth and David are picking through flood rubble. (David's found the top half of a small water pump, which he finds amusing enough to send his glasses almost off his nose.) Farmers in Fallon receive some of the most heavily subsidized water in the country to grow alfalfa, one of our more thirsty crops, at the southern end of the 40 Mile Desert, the most ferociously arid stretch of the emigrant trail crossing the West to California. They then cut, bale, and ship the stuff on trucks over the Sierra, at no small cost in fossil fuel, to ranchers in California—where same said ranchers receive federal subsidies to *not* grow alfalfa. That's the third screwy reallocation of nature-based resources I've noted in two days, and on that note we leave in order to finish the freeway portion of the drive so we can get down to brass tacks, or the tactics of the brass, as it were. If Fallon loses its farmers, it still has the military to rely upon for economic sustenance.

Twelve contrails crisscross the light aqua sky as we drive through Painted Rock, a roadcut as colorful as it sounds, the artificial cliffs held in place with chain link fence. The amount of woven wire draped across vertical acres of loose rock and dirt is on such a large scale that the fence looks as if it's draped softly on the hills. The first sign for Las Vegas appears, as does the third road kill of the morning, a skunk.

The land and sky here seem to take a deep breath together and hold

9:00 A.M.: Fernley We come out of the canyon and into prime ranchland, which has slowly been sold off during the last decade to make room for spreading bedroom subdivisions serving Reno, then climb up a hill and into the desert proper. The land and sky here seem to take a deep breath together and hold it, opening up to the vast interior dryness of the basin. The Truckee turns sharply left and north to continue on to Pyramid Lake, taking what greenery there is with it, while we continue east to the second Fernley exit where we leave the interstate. Now we're on Alternate 50, a feeder to that mythical two-lane blacktop US 50, dubbed "the Loneliest Highway in America." Parallel-ing both the irrigation ditch and the railroad, the highway this morning is anything but lonely; pickups are on their way to church while RVs begin their daily search for a scenic climax.

A few miles east and topping a small rise, the road bends gently to the right and passes what's left of Hazen, a dusty grocery store and nearby "antique" stall sitting at elevation 4,004 feet. Hazen used to be a small railroad town, and in 1904 housed enough workers on the Newlands project to merit a post office. Now it's on its way to joining the more than five hundred other towns that have died in Nevada during the last century and a quarter. Most towns in Nevada don't last as long as an average human lifetime, and Hazen, settled just after the Civil War, has managed to beat the average. From here to Fallon, the road skirts the lower edge of the Carson Sink.

To drive from Reno to Las Vegas is to feel as if you're a message vibrating along a string between two tin cans. There's a close connection between the two places, but it's definitely low tech, all but forgotten when the two towns outgrew each others' friendship. In 1959 when I moved to Reno, its popula-tion of 50,000 still exceeded that of Las Vegas, and for years the political power in Carson City's legislative roundhouse was held by Reno and the rural counties. By the 1990s, Reno's citizenry could maybe be stretched to 150,000—but Las Vegas was fast closing in on the one million mark and had all but completely rebalanced the powers of state government. And US 95, the most direct route between the two cities, couldn't help bridge the gap of economic envy and political frustration. In fact, the highway doesn't even pass through Reno, but sixty miles to the east in Fallon.

9:23 A.M.: Fallon Nine miles west of town the main branch of US 50 joins in from Carson City, and the architecture begins to take on that same distinctive format it demonstrates north of Kingman: doublewides anchored in yards of junk. Out here it's not unattractive and makes perfect sense, the modest dwellings embedded in vernacular environments where the rust and miscellaneous colored rocks are arranged in patterns that are almost legible. It's not folk art—that would be too pretentious a name for it—but a casual accumulation of stuff that nonetheless is organized by loose categories: car doors go here, old boards to the left, red rocks in front, and green ones to the side. That sort of thing. On our right sits the forsaken drive-in movie theater, a commonly accepted cautionary emblem of post-1960s rural America, the screen which held our projected hopes and fantasies now full of holes.

Between these outposts of detritus and downtown is a creeping infill of strip malls and fast food joints, most of which are welcomed by the locals. The red and orange plastic signs and tilt-up walls may be ugly, but it beats a two-hour round trip into Reno to buy a pizza, or so the reasoning goes. It's time to eat the breakfast we skipped in Reno, and after circling through town once to check the alternatives, we choose the Depot casino, which used to have a decent coffeeshop. The temperature is up to 47 degrees and David sheds his coat, the inside of the Honda beginning to resemble the large and messy nest of a North American raptor. In addition to the usual stack of maps, atlases, and guidebooks, the binoculars, sunglasses, and cooler, we've added David's notebooks, pouches, reading and writing materials, and a second spare coat. It's comfortable, though a little cramped, and we'll take turns alternating David in and out of the back seat so he can stretch out once in a while.

Inside the Depot it's all dark carpeting and low ceilings, fake railroad signs and stale cigarette smoke. A guy in a cowboy hat at the bar contemplates a half-empty beer, while two elderly ladies yank determinedly on quarter slots. The only other customer among the hundred or so machines is a kid working a video poker machine. He's just old enough to have cultivated a small colony of hairs on his upper lip and looks more like he's still playing a video game in an arcade than gambling.

Beth claims a table by the window, a hard-voiced blonde already moving in with her coffee pot. She starts to ask if we want some, takes a look at my face and says *Never mind,* and just starts pouring. I look out the window for a quick traffic count. The dominant vehicle is the pickup truck, most commonly a Ford F150, the name of which always reminds me of fighter jets, an appropriate enough reaction in Fallon, which hosts the largest naval air station in the Western Hemisphere. The second most noticeable cars are late-model American muscle cars, your white Trans Ams, red or black Firebirds, and 5.0 Mustangs in all colors. Top gun wranglers from nearby ranches mingle in the traffic with Top Gun fighter jockeys from the base, the former in pickups, the latter in the cars, identical sets of hormones parading horsepower up and down the street, even on Sunday morning. It's amusing until you think of the young fighter pilots flying around in supersonic sports cars loaded with enough munitions to take out downtown Reno in one pass.

Breakfast comes and goes, an unmemorable collection of eggs and pancakes, but the coffee keeps pouring until we're ready to leave. David's been analyzing the signs that decorate the place, deciding that there are actually some real railroad signs interspersed with the copies, an infiltration of the local and the genuine into the imported simulacra. Outside, the air is fresh and cool, the morning continuing to warm, and I turn over the keys to Beth, who quickly and efficiently gets headed south on US 95, the road to Las Vegas. Before leaving town we pass a house with a flooded yard, several geese paddling around.

Straight and with a progressively higher speed posted as we enter the farm-lands, we level off at the new legal limit, 70 mph. We're surprised, given that it's only a two-lane road. New Mexico has kept its two-lane highways capped at 55 and California at 65, both states only letting the interstates go any higher at 75. It's a realistic speed for this road, though, given the distance between towns and the long stretches of straight and level blacktop. You stand more danger of killing yourself while driving to Las Vegas by falling asleep at 55 than you do by hitting something at 70.

The fields south of town are flooded, all the ditches full. When I last drove through here on my way to Santa Fe in the fall of 1993 this was all dust, and they were able to get only two cuttings of alfalfa that year out of an optimum of five. There's water for the moment, though, and assuming the spring runoff doesn't keep everything submerged for half the year, once again they'll be pulling handsome crops out of here in the summer. It's going to be a short-lived renaissance, however, unless the global weather patterns revert to the Pleistocene moisture of 10,000 years ago when this was a wetlands.

The fields end, and now it's sagebrush that's flooded. At the far end of the valley the road climbs up toward Russell Pass and we sight the "Top Gun Drag Strip," which presumably means a place to race cars and not F-18s, its dirt track about the only dry piece of level ground we can see. On the other side of the pass, the landscape to the east unfolds in a series of hazy ridges. The nearest peaks, the Blow Sand Mountains, are within the purview of the naval air station, and signs arrayed along the road warn of "Low Flying Air-craft." It's a caution found throughout Nevada, though a trifle insufficient when a jet flies a hundred feet over your car at night firing rockets at a target a few hundred yards off the road, as happens in Dixie Valley just east of Fallon.

Over 80 percent of Nevada is owned by the federal government, and 16 per-cent of the entire country's military lands are within the state, some four mil-lion acres in all. Superlatives accumulate: Fallon is not only the largest naval air station in the West, but the largest electronic warfare range in the world.

While Nevada is the most urban state in the union, with well over 85 percent of its population living in or adjacent to Reno or Las Vegas, its landscape is also the most militarized. Nellis Air Force Range, the largest peacetime military ground and airspace in the Western world, is three million acres on the ground with control over more than ten million acres of airspace, a territory that's been compared in size to Switzerland. The military drops bombs out here, shoots off rockets and airborne cannon rounds, and fires lasers (one of the nearby "Warning: Approved Laser Range" signs was once involuntarily donated to our family art collection). From here to Las Vegas the military installations are a patchwork terrain of forbidden parcels either within sight or close by and just over a hill.

We cross the boundary of the Walker River Indian Reservation, and the top of Mt. Grant, at 11,239 feet the highest point of the Wassuk Range, comes into view. It's always impressive to see the peak, which looms over Walker Lake and the town of Hawthorn, two features still hidden from view. First we have to pass through Schurz, elevation 4,126 feet, which we reach at 10:54 A.M., diving into the cool green of the cottonwoods lining the very full Walker River. On the other side of the bridge this morning, both of the Nevada Highway Patrol cars responsible for all of west-central Nevada are parked in front of the local restaurant, the officers presumably meeting over coffee. David points out that the nearby Church of Latter Day Saints is a mobile home, while Beth directs my attention to four guys wearing baseball caps and sweatshirts sitting in a boat parked to one side of the house next door. Maybe they're waiting for the really Big Flood, having the means for both spiritual and bodily salvation at hand. Except for the trees growing alongside the Walker River, everything in town looks ready to pick up and move.

The road climbs over a short rise, then soon dips into the Walker Lake basin, which holds one of the most supremely surreal earthworks on the planet. Looming under a high thin scrim of gray cloud to our right is Mt. Grant, much closer now, and the birthplace of the Ghost Dance, that late nineteenth-century visionary Indian cult that foretold the expulsion of white men from the continent. Sweeping above and below us are eleven stepped terraces, ancient beaches from the prehistoric times demonstrating all too vividly the slow death of the lake. And in front us, covering 147,000 acres, are arrayed the bunkers of the largest ammunition depot in the hemisphere, if not the entire world. We pull off the road above the lake, David uncorking himself from the back seat with a slewing sideways motion that almost produces an audible Pop! of relief as he squeezes out. Except for the occasional vehicle passing by, it's entirely silent.

The rim of Walker Lake at this point is defined by 20 Mile Beach, a camping and boating shore that remains popular with fishing parties—or will remain popular until the fish are gone. The lake level had dropped almost a hundred feet between 1930 and 1994, a quarter of the shrinkage taking place just since 1976, the combined effect of continual drought and serious overcommitment of the water rights in the Walker River system. The rapidly increasing salinity of the remaining water was supposed to kill off the last of the fish no later than the year 2000, but the three wet winters have given them a reprieve. As it is for the majority of the farmers around Fallon, it's a losing battle for the cutthroat trout, but this morning David counts two dozen boats with fishermen in just our quadrant of the lake.

Descending three of the shoreline benches in about twenty yards, down to the edge of a particularly steep drop off to the next terrace, we turn and slowly pick our way back to the car in a more or less straight line, inventorying the litter as we go. Despite that fact we've picked a small and inconspicuous pullout, the survey results are impressive: four rusted tin cans, fourteen broken bottles, one plastic drink top, a dried orange peel, and one toddler's size tennis shoe; a foot-long section of truck tire (tread in good condition), one gas cap, one Brisk Iced Tea plastic bottle, a Budweiser can, and a transparent blue plastic lighter with fuel (which sparks but doesn't light); two empty motor oil jugs (Castrol 20W-50W), one tire inflator/sealant can (empty), one Salem cigarette pack (empty), one blue straw (same color as the lighter), two Polaroid film packs (empty); and two copies of a receipt with carbon from the American Building Company in Carson City for "13 out of 182 of part #95212, 33′0″ long."

What this quick roadside archeology reveals is a cross-section of the traffic by the lake, from families traveling with their children to truckers hauling pipe, from old cars overheating on the grades to tourists in RVs stopping for a smoke and a beer. Back on the shoulder most of the junk is hidden, slowly subsiding into the ground and forming a new layer within the geology for future reading.

11:38 A.M.: Hawthorne Two miles south a sheriff has a Range Rover with California plates pulled over. The entrance to the beach below displays, according to David, about one hundred recreational vehicles in various stages of disarray for the weekend. On a nearby boulder a fresh Valentine has been painted, its red heart outlined in white tracery, almost too nice to label as graffiti, and then we're on the edge of the Hawthorne Army Ammunition Depot. Parked as a decoy at the boundary is a decommissioned black-and-white, the retired patrol car resting on low tires. Signs instruct explosive-laden trucks to avoid the main gate of the base, and Beth prudently drops a little speed.

Hawthorne was a railroad town in the late 1800s, has been an on-again off-again county seat since 1883, and nearly burned to the ground in 1926. It might have simply become another sandy beach at the southern end of the lake but for its selection that same year to become a safely remote site for the storage of bombs, hand grenades, mines, bullets, artillery shells, and mustard gas. Subsequently, the town's economy has been almost totally dependent on the fortunes of war, thriving when the ammo trade is in full swing during conflicts, and shrinking in between. In the mid-1980s things looked pretty dismal, and all the depot did was store weapons and run a salvage and demilitarization operation dismantling munitions. The end of the Cold War early the next decade could have again killed the town, but lately, due to the budget cutting of the bipartisan Base Realignment and Closure Commission, the Hawthorne Depot has been receiving relocated munitions from bases being closed in Oregon, Arizona, and New Mexico, states which are apparently held in greater scenic esteem than central Nevada.

To the east, dozens of newly painted yellow army freight cars with bright red doors are parked on sidings, perhaps evidence of fresh deliveries. Information about the depot is notoriously difficult to obtain, so we're not sure. To our west the crisply laid out officer's houses with their rectangular lawns and empty flagpoles are occupied by local residents. The depot is now run by a civilian contractor and only two military personnel are on site, but the integration of the town and military remains evident by the cemetery, where a dozen large artillery casings and a double-barreled antiaircraft gun mark the entrance to downtown, such as it is. The bars, casinos, markets, and gas stations in Hawthorne are remarkable only for their lack of distinction, a quasi-urban architecture with only the smallest pretense to anything other than factual signage. In a reversal of the normal order of things, the built environment of the town is overshadowed by the military signage, and once through town, the extent of the bunkers becomes apparent.

High and steeply graded parallelograms of dirt, many with sagebrush growing on their sides, most of the "igloos," as they're designated by the army, are bisected at both ends by driveways cut down to ground level. The bunkers themselves have large metal loading doors at either end, which face concrete blast shields built into the dirt across the driveways. We park off the road by one of the numerous and seemingly undefended entrances to the base, and I ask both Beth and David to estimate the number of bunkers in the valley. Stretching in every direction into the foothills, the relentless and very visible military grid of dirt roads and two hundred miles of railroad tracks makes apparent how large the valley really is, how immense the territory we're traversing today.

Beth shakes her head, speechless. David gropes for a number—*1,000—2,000—5,000?* None of us can guess. It takes a printout from the Center for Land Use Interpretation in Los Angeles to inform us that there are 2,427 of the igloos with a storage capacity exceeding 7.6 million square feet, that as of March 1996 was 74 percent utilized.

We're about to leave when we realize that the gate in front of us leads into the "N.U.W.C. Detachment." Putting a "Naval Underwater Warfare Center" at a lake everyone knows is drying up rapidly seems a bit odd. A model of the submarine USS *Nevada,* fashioned from an old torpedo and painted matte black, acts as a mascot to one side, while on the other a large sign warn us that photographing, sketching, or taking notes about this facility is strictly forbidden, that everyone is subject to search at any time, and persons caught violating the rules will be subject to prosecution. There's also a polite request to leave all matches and lighters with security personnel at the gate, none of whom are in evidence. Just outside the sentry post a white sign reading "Threat Condition" has the word "Normal" in green letters attached to it, an odd parody of forest fire warning signs throughout the West. We give up trying to decipher any of this and drive off, only to come to a screeching U-turn thirty seconds later when one of the blue Adopt-a-Road signs catches my eye. Underneath, the name of the sponsor is listed as the "*Nuclear* Underwater Warfare Center," which carries with it a distinctly different and more ominous meaning than simply "Naval." We wonder which one is correct.

As we leave the valley, Beth still driving and David writing furiously in his journal, I turn to catch a last glimpse of Mt. Grant. Despite the fact that it's within the jurisdiction of the military, which appropriated the peak to protect the depot from attacks launched off higher ground, and that there's a dirt road leading to the top, I've always wanted to hike it. It's not that I would expect to reexperience the vision of Wovoka, the Paiute prophet of the Ghost Dance, but to be physically on the site out of which such a powerful story emanated is always sobering. It's a very nearly apocryphal metaphor for the summit—

where Wovoka supposedly received his visions of the whites being consumed by cataclysm—that it is included by the military within their largest preserve of explosives.

David agrees with me that the depot outdoes any other example of large-scale geo-forming we've ever seen, and I reminisce how driving through it when I was sixteen prepared me to embrace wholly the earthworks by Robert Smithson and Michael Heizer when I first saw photographs of them in the early 1970s. I still wonder how Jim Turrell has been affected by Hawthorne, an artist who as a small plane pilot has flown over most of the West, able to see not only from the ground, but also from the air, how the military has massively revised the geography of the region. The same is true for de Maria, whose "*Lightning Field*" in New Mexico lays out a grid to attract the immense explosions of lightning. I was speculating during the drive from Santa Fe to Las Vegas about the redemptive gestures of these artists in relationship to the federally mandated viewpoints in national parks, but Hawthorne makes clear that they also play off the rearranging of the landscape perpetrated by the military. Jeff Kelley continues to this day to describe Heizer's "*Complex One,*" a piece located practically within shouting range of the Test Site, as a bunker facing the nuclear blasts, and has wondered for twenty years about the possible connection between its shape and the igloos in Hawthorne.

At about noon we leave the boundary of the depot and a sign announces a dust hazard. Given that there's standing water next to the road, perhaps it's not as serious a threat today as on some others. This section of the drive, through flat valleys and playas, is visually bereft of artifacts to count, except for the telephone poles. David stretches out as far as he can in the back seat, about an extra three inches, narrows his eyes, logs in our speed, and starts counting. *Three hundred feet,* he announces a few minutes later.

What? Beth and I both ask.

Three hundred feet, that's how far apart the poles are. And did you notice

6. Michael Heizer, *Complex One,* east-central Nevada, 1972–74. Concrete, steel, and compacted earth, 23 ft. 6 in. by 140 ft. by 110 ft. Photograph © 1991 by Michael Heizer.

how the centerline reflectors around Hawthorne were only twenty feet apart, like one-third the normal interval, I guess because they really don't want you drifting in front of those munitions trucks?

Beth and I look at each other, thinking: David is absolutely unreal. He's not only counting, but establishing periodicity elements in the landscape and working out the reasons why. I shake my head and write it all down (22 poles per minute at 72 mph, etc.) before we come into Luning, which lies at the northern end of Soda Spring Valley.

Another mining town that boomed in the 1800s and then busted early the next century, it's a prime example of how the desert strips a settlement so far down beneath even the barest functionality that it achieves a fundamental existence more akin to art than architecture. David comments that it looks as if the junkyard organizes itself into houses at its periphery. I think that's exactly right. The joint ventures of mining and railroad produced not a town but a junkyard, and out of that concatenation arose dwellings. The tiny frame houses with frayed screen porches are surrounded by a maternal hierarchy of junk, akin to but sublimely beyond anything we saw around Fallon. There's romance in rust, as every school kid who collects it and every artist who works in assemblage knows. Rust verges on being inscrutable, tantalizes us

Rust verges on being inscrutable, tantalizes

with clues as to what "took place" here. Rusted junk is the American counterpart to Europe's ruins, and pieces of it can appeal to the collector in all of us almost as much as an arrowhead or fragment of an Anasazi pot.

Abruptly we're through the town and back on the flat, headed toward Mina at the southern end of the valley. The playa is so narrow and barren that your eyes cease to distinguish individual features through color, relying exclusively on boundary definition and shape. Dirt roads stand out as significant geometry, leading the eye upward to the old mines. The telephone poles keep cadence in the flat light, the overcast slowly thickening as we drive. Just before Mina we spy the peaks at the northern end of the White Mountains on the border with California. Rising up over 14,000 feet and covered in snow, they're a startling visual release between the brown desert and the flat sky. A band of aqua hovers above the Owens Valley on the other side of the range, and it's everything David can do to return his eyes to the road, so alluring is the presence of color.

Five ravens circle over the "city" limits of Mina, elevation 4,540 feet, no population listed. Highway 95 morphs into Front Street with a sign that says "No Explosive Laden Vehicles to Park in Town," a warning also posted outside Luning, as Beth reminds me. Mina must have the highest degree of entropy evident in any town in America. The Nevada poet Gary Short has it right when he writes in "Near Mina:" "On the outskirts of town / a crop / of abandoned cars." The rust here is positively organic, it's so prolific, and David notes that even the places that are open (we think two) look closed. It's a beautiful pair of towns, Luning and Mina, though I wouldn't want to live in them anymore than I would inside a sculpture by those masters of twentieth-century assemblage, Edward and Nancy Reddin Kienholz.

This is an aesthetic I understand, having grown up in the desert where junk

th clues as to what "took place" here.

is highly visible, and it's the logical artistic extension of simply collecting the stuff. Developed by the Kienholzes and their peers in California during the mid-twentieth century, it's a subspecies of sculpture where the rusted bits and pieces of automotive culture are combined with discarded mannequins, cast-off appliances, and all manner of domestic and industrial refuse into sometimes nostalgic, sometimes sordid shrines to sexual longing and the escape from death and dying. The ruins of Luning and Mina should be declared intact as sites on the National Register of the American Imagination, not just for historical value, but also as vivid examples of the half-life of civilization. We're tempted to stop, to take a more careful measure, but we're barely on schedule to make a dinner at the Beckmanns' in Las Vegas, so we keep moving. At the edge of town another black-and-white squats in the weeds, marking some unknown symmetry with its partner to the north. Beth speeds up over the limit and kicks in the cruise control.

We tick off landmarks on the maps and in our notes: Billie's Massage & Sauna with its two prefabs tricked out in red trim, another mostly functional architecture with its unambiguous signage; Rhodes with its salt marsh, where camels imported from North Africa were used to transport salt to the silver mills a hundred miles away; a concrete ruin with Cyndee, Ashley, Tonya, Carey, and Holly inscribed against the wind that now blows alkali off the flat. The cars, trucks, and RVs have evened out in a one-to-one-to-one ratio. We pass over the unremarkable Redlich Summit, then descend to Coaldale Junction where our road curves east, away from the White Mountains and the snow, the alluring patch of blue sky still there, and head toward Tonopah. For the first time we see pedestrians alongside the road, one guy in camo, the other carrying a pack, both headed toward the gas station at the junction. They don't look particularly concerned.

To the north and east of us the 10,000-foot-high ridges of the Shoshone, Toiyabe, Toquima, and Monitor ranges form the great running walls of the Reese River, Big Smoky and Monitor valleys, the heart of the state. The scale along this part of the drive is hard to grasp, almost hallucinatory, and twenty miles feels like an hour, as if we're crawling slowly through a still photograph. The highway makes a great semicircle around Lone Mountain, a 9,000-foot peak surrounded on all sides by alkali flats, then passes the Crescent Sand Dunes off in the distance to the left before rising into Tonopah and the most thoroughly disturbed landscape I know. Old silver mine tailings, their sides streaked with corrosive minerals, have been gouged by runoff from thunderstorms; new lengths of white PVC pipe are stuck everywhere into the ground like straws, the claim markers of Japanese and Canadian mining conglomerates.

SIX

1:38 P.M.: Tonopah—halfway Entering the town at elevation 6,030 feet on its
northern edge, and leaving it at 6,256 on the southern, where the road goes
over the Tonopah Summit, this is the highest point of our drive all day, not on
a wilderness mountain pass, but in the middle of a mining town. Situated on
the side of the modest San Antonio Range, the terrain is riddled with tunnels,
shafts, pits, and roads, its peaks covered with microwave towers, radio antennae, and radar domes. Overlaid among and literally on top of the nineteenth-
century town are the rental units, gas stations, and supermarkets thrown up
during the 1970s and 1980s to cope with the most recent boomlets in gold
and molybdenum mining.

The place is a mess, but with great character. A dome house sits imperi-
ously near prefabs; ticky-tacky apartments lean up against sturdy square-cut
stone buildings, and the restored turn-of-the-century Mitzpah Hotel rises
across the street from an almost comic 1960's populuxe motel. All the rust
seems arranged in suitably photogenic poses, the former glories of the mining
camp in convenient display. Tonopah is one of those places that inspires casino architects into romancing the ruins of the mining culture from the last
century. There's nothing fancy about the town, but it's rife with irresistible
fictions. Howard Hughes got married here, the air force furtively pitted
Stealth bombers against captured Soviet MIGs at night overhead, and more
than one Nevada governor has had assignations in town. It's hot in the summer, ridiculously cold and windy in winter, and the few trees in town seem to
cower through it all.

It's time to rotate positions in the car, so we stop at the Texaco Food Mart
and regress into childhood. This cannot be blamed solely on the nature of

road trips, which call for the suspension of all adult logic in any case; the real reason is collusion among the corporate minimarts across America to make sure we stay consumerist teenagers forever. The last time I had Cornuts, for instance, was during junior high school. David buys a bag. Beth opts for some gooey chocolate and caramel thing she remembers eating as a kid in Illinois, as well as a hefty bag of Sun Chips, one of her essential food groups. Eying the Hostess cupcakes, I narrowly achieve a moral victory and instead buy a protein bar.

Once outside, we rearrange the car, Beth in back for a nap after her snacks, David in the passenger seat with maps and binoculars, and me driving. We pull out just ahead of a long string of RVs and beat them to the summit. It's all downhill from here to Las Vegas, 200 miles south. I tuck my virtuous fat-free snack into the glove compartment and dive gleefully into the Cornuts with David.

2:03 P.M.: Goldfield Passengers on commercial jets flying between Reno and Las Vegas in the early 1980s, had they a current aviation chart in their laps and the flight path been just right, would have noticed a curious anomaly. Just south and east of Tonopah, barely visible over a range and within the boundaries of the off-limits airspace of the Nellis Air Force Base, was a very long, very recently paved, very black airstrip. The aviation chart, however, would note only an old World War II landing strip long since abandoned. We can't see it from the road, but that's where the Stealths and MIGs were flown until a few years ago. From now until we're in Las Vegas we'll be within sight of Nellis, the borders of which sometimes touch the road and are never more than a few miles to the east.

The northwest corner of the base squares off in the middle of Mud Lake, which we pass going almost ninety on the straight and level between Tonopah and Goldfield. To the west, as we descend from the summit, we can see briefly through a break in the White Mountains over to a long portion of the southern

Sierra, I think from roughly the Palisades down to Mt. Whitney. That view quickly disappears, and I turn my attention back to the left and Nellis.

Here comes that old feeling that's haunted me ever since a I was child: Look, over there, where it's empty—see how the light shines just over that hill. Couldn't we, shouldn't we just go and take a look?

And, of course, it's a feeling that comes only when you're prevented from getting to where it is you're looking, either because you lack the time or means to get there, or because it's forbidden. Nellis has for me the same attraction as Tibet or Iceland. It's not impossible to get there, just highly unlikely, and that irks me. Beth and David are staring quietly in the same direction, yearning plainly visible on their faces. They pass the binoculars back and forth, as if they could somehow see through the hills, over the buffer zone provided by the base and into the Test Site itself, the most remote portion of which lies behind the Cactus Range. That's where they used to let off the largest underground tests at the site, the huge subsidence craters clearly visible in satellite photos of the area.

Just past Mud Lake, halfway to Goldfield, the first Joshua trees appear, that vegetable anomaly scientists classify as either an agave or a lily. It doesn't especially look like either, so that's no help, its shaggy limbs and uplifted spiky pompoms declaiming an alien piety. They're a perfect plant to accompany Nellis, adding to the air of strangeness experienced when traveling next to forbidden territory.

Running uphill and slowed by a semi in front of us, we come into Goldfield, once the largest city in Nevada. More than 10,000 people lived in Goldfield in 1907, while today the town holds perhaps 400 out of the county's entire population of only 1,300. Like most rural counties in Nevada, the population density is so low here that it falls under the two-person-per-square-mile limit that defined the official American frontier during the nineteenth century. Because it was once so prominent and is still physically standing, and because the active highway runs through the middle of it,

Goldfield is the most memorable example of boom and bust in the state. This is painfully apparent in the starkly handsome stone and brick buildings scattered up and down the street, including the Goldfield Hotel, the county courthouse, and the high school. I've never met anyone who's driven through Goldfield who's not lamented the abandonment of those buildings, some of the most substantial historical architecture in Nevada. Several attempts have been made to renovate the hotel, but all have failed for lack of sufficient funds. And even if any had succeeded, how would they have kept open their doors? There's not enough local population to fill the bar, the tourists are too busy getting from one end of 95 to the other, and Tonopah's more nearly the middle of the trip for a break.

While it's easy to grasp the economics behind the slow disintegration of Goldfield, it fails to resolve the emotions evoked by the town for most passersby, and the buildings become like the Joshua trees, mute totems in a land that fascinates us, but where we're essentially strangers. Weaving around the semi where there's room, we keep going uphill and over the pass on the other side of town, elevation 6,087, our second highest point, then resume the downhill run.

This business of being a stranger, of estrangement, is underscored for the three of us as we head farther south. David fusses with the Nevada and California maps, as well as the Nevada atlas, trying to determine which mountain range is which. We're close to Lida Junction, the turnoff to Deep Springs where a very small, very liberal arts college is located that he attended over two decades ago. He's not been this close to Deep Springs in thirteen years, and he's trying desperately to get a fix on his memories, allied as all of ours are to specific places.

The basin and range here is complicated, wrinkled, folded, and contains dozens of mountain chains: are we looking at the Silver Peak Range, or the Slate Range? Are those the Grapevine or the Last Chance mountains? Is that the high ridge of the White Mountains, or have we gone far enough south that it's now the Inyo's? It takes patience, reading the topography, matching it to the maps, integrating everything into a coherent picture of place that is capable of evoking memories. But David does it, slowly ordering the geography feature by feature into the sequence of our travel, which in turn allows him to call up stories from his college days that he can then tell us.

That's why the estrangement factor is important. When we're in a place where the land itself is strange to us, we have no memory of it. I don't mean simply traveling to somewhere we've not visited before; that's not so difficult. Most of the places we visit, even if we've never been there before, we recognize. Either we've seen pictures of it, been told stories or read about it, or the landscape just falls into a category we've experienced elsewhere, so there's some preexisting familiarity. Most of the Great Basin, and in particular big sections of it in Nevada, are outside our normal scope of familiarity. For instance, conventional wisdom has it that when you're lost, follow water downstream and you'll eventually cross a road or hit civilization. In the Great Basin, all the water flows inward either to evaporate or to become groundwater. Following water downhill can strand you dying of thirst on the edge of a salt flat. We've had this problem ever since we encountered the American deserts, misnaming even its most common plants and animals, a habit of mind we maintain today. Most people still think a horned toad is a toad, but it's a lizard, and the yucca tree isn't a tree. Such misnaming is an attempt to frame the desert in terms we understand, to equate its features with those we know in other places, a strategy doomed, for the most part, to humorous failure, though sometimes the results are fatal.

This last summer and about two mountain ranges west, in the northern part of Death Valley National Park (and just one valley south of Deep Springs), a German family of four drove off the edge of that strangeness and disappeared. Their rental car was found on a dirt road, all four tires flat to their rims and obviously driven, literally, into the ground. It looked to the rangers as if the family had turned off the main road to go exploring, gotten a flat or two, and assumed that if they kept going they'd find people. Wrong assumption. The next mistake they made was to leave the car; empty cans were found a bit farther down the road—and that's all. As of now, I've not heard that anyone has discovered what happened to them.

This isn't something that happened during an emigrant crossing of the last century, but in 1996 in a national park that saw 1.2 million visitors last year. The reason it happened is that the Germans had no previous experience with anything like the Great Basin; the rules here are different, and even water, that most basic and common element of survival found anywhere in the world, doesn't act like it does in your home territory. The strangeness is also, of course, exactly why there's a Death Valley National Park and the Mojave National Preserve. It's the reason why winter snowbirds take their RVs out along the length of US 50 a bit farther north—to be able to claim, with pride, that they survived a piece of the desert myth. And strangeness defines the exact character of this road as compared to the drives from Santa Fe and Los Angeles.

Driving west from Santa Fe to Las Vegas is to follow westward the American dream toward California. It's a route exactly as much traveled and well marked in our imagination as in our history, and we have the souvenir trading posts to prove it, a sentimental knickknack for every cliché of the journey, whether it's fake arrowheads, clumps of fool's gold, or postcards of jackalope, an animal that for all practical purposes might just as well exist, so confused are we about the nature of pronghorn antelope and jackrabbits. Wallace Stegner points out that in reality the former are more goat than antelope, and the latter aren't even technically rabbits. But at least in New Mexico and Arizona we've known how to exist, how to farm and ranch and form communities.

The road from Los Angeles to Las Vegas is at one level simply traveling in reverse the second half of that old trail from Santa Fe to southern California. Where it crosses the Mojave, the southernmost extension of the Great Basin, it's known as the most dangerous portion of the trip. But it's also a quintessential example of that prime characteristic of the West: it's a place of transit, a place merely to get through on the way somewhere else. Only recently and reluctantly has it suffered much settlement, population driven there by hyperescalating property values in greater Los Angeles. If the road from Santa Fe is characterized by our collective romantic memory of the nineteenth century, the road from L.A. is a scene out of the movies, a flight into the night on the way to Vegas where we can loosen our ties, belts, and other inhibitions.

The road from Reno is a whole other order of business. Going from north to south, it's not a route anchored, as are the other western trails, in our history of westward expansion. It didn't carry emigrants from the East going to California. It stays within the basin, doesn't escape to a kinder, gentler landscape. It's not a road we associate with the movies, anymore than we tend to link Nevada with traditional tales of cowboys and Indians, which in the simplicities of popular culture tend always to inhabit Arizona or Texas or Montana, anywhere but Nevada. No, the road from Reno is not familiar to the national consciousness, is only two lanes, and defines itself to us through estrangement from our perceptions. No wonder divorce first became an industry in Reno at one end, and the hallucination we label Las Vegas was built at the other.

The emotion I feel when driving this road is longing. I want to know the unknown, to cross every range and peer down into every basin. Traveling through Nevada is to cross one of those rare physical manifestations of the Void, the Big Empty, a nearby corner of the universe we haven't yet filled up with suburbs, exit ramps, day-care centers, and wholesale auto tire warehouses. It's as close to outer space as I'm going to get, an illusion made all the more real by the science-fiction presence of radar domes in Tonopah and NASA tracking antennae farther down the road, by military hardware and the lunar-like tailings of cyanide leaching ponds.

All this serious rumination is broken momentarily as we pass through Lida Junction, the windsock at the airstrip for the Cottontail Ranch flapping gaily in the breeze. Another one of Nevada's more infamous whorehouses and the subject of many jokes at Deep Springs, the junction being a convenient drop-off point for students arriving and departing by bus, its madam once ran for governor of the state. Perhaps the strangest part of the campaign is that she didn't get very far! The little cluster of prefabs is one of the few artifacts of note on this stretch of the road, and once past it David and I turn back to brooding separately over the landscape while Beth curls up for a nap in the back. We stay on our southerly bearing, turning slightly east toward Scotty's Junction where the road from Death Valley comes in, the road so bereft of anything classifiable as a scenic attraction that even the guidebook doesn't have anything to say about it.

2:59 P.M.: Beatty Just outside Beatty by a few minutes, David notices the creosote bushes. I can't say for sure that this is their most northern appearance next to the road, having zoned out for a few miles in contemplation of nothing in particular, a calming of thoughts most welcome after attempting to see and record everything I can (and knowing from experience this time how much I'm missing). The spindly dark bushes define the boundary of the Mojave Desert, as opposed to the higher and drier Great Basin desert—sort of. The definitions of the Great Basin are numerous and sometimes contradictory. The hydrographic and most inclusive definition, which I prefer because it's based on the inflow of water, contains most of the Mojave. On the other hand, if you're tracing its boundaries by plant community, as a biologist will, the floristic Great Basin is dominated by sagebrush and other plants tolerant of a climate colder than the other deserts, while the Mojave is signified by the creosote bush, which only grows under 4,000 feet elevation, and is a sure sign that we're steadily losing altitude. Sure enough, Beatty sits at 3,300 feet.

Our approach from the north skirts the eastern edge of the Bullfrog Hills and runs through Oasis Valley, the first consistently green area we've seen since the cottonwoods in Schurz. Well, almost green. The fields and semimarshy area down by the intermittent stream are not exactly bursting with spring yet, but there's enough evidence of chlorophyll that we sit up a little straighter. Horses are pastured to our left, and at times I've seen wild burros grazing alongside them. Not today, though. US 95 makes its sharpest curves at both ends of Beatty for a hundred miles in either direction, and the transition from the valley to town is marked by a wrecked airplane. If my war movie lore serves me right, it's a vintage DC-3 that's propped up in the weeds and slightly reminiscent of the two sheriff cars left out on the desert to the north. It's been here at least since I was a poet-in-residence in the local schools for two weeks during the winter of 1973 or 1974, and I've always half-wondered if the pilot was following the road and became confused by the curve, which bends around the old dirt airstrip. In any case we, too, are going to touch down, more gently I hope, and fuel up. I pull off into the first of the three stations in town and Beth stirs groggily in the back. David gets out, windmills his arms, and rotates his neck a few times.

Beatty is reasonably prosperous and the junk, which is to say decay, is held to a minimum. Apart from the huge gold mine south of town, the reason why is surrounding us at the pumps. Two BMW touring bikes with Nevada plates are just topping off when a Honda Goldwing wobbles in. We're talking big yuppie bucks here for recreational weekend touring, couples from Las Vegas passing through Beatty for a spin around Death Valley, the entrance for which is only six miles west. Beatty sells a lot of gas. A Porsche Carrara convertible pulls in as the BMW leaves, followed closely by two of its less expensive cousins, a pair of 944's. Beatty is the first town any distance north of Las Vegas, and the nearby ghost town of Ryolite is more or less on the way to Death Valley, enough of a scenic excuse for a Sunday drive. Stopping for gas during summer weekdays, sometimes I've caught a couple of large unmarked semis pulled up at one of the stations, accompanied by cars that look vaguely like they belong in the Mercedes-Benz family, but with radically altered sheet metal and unfamiliar headlight configurations. They did, in fact, belong to the German automaker, which sent them out here for field testing during the height of desert heat, a not uncommon use of both US 95 and the national park.

Beth and David are waiting in line to use the bathrooms, and after paying the cashier I pull the car off to one side to catalog the traffic, which now comprises mostly recreational drivers. Beatty used to be a much sleepier town twenty-five years ago, a place I much enjoyed when I was doing my two-week stint as a poet-in-the-schools for the Nevada State Council on the Arts. Residents were a little puzzled by, one, what a poet exactly was and, two, what such a person was doing with their kids. After a series of workshops the first week with my partner in the program, Dan McCrimmon, a songwriter/guitarist from Denver, the kids produced hundreds of stories and poems about the town and their parents, the desert and how their dreams for adulthood did or did not include Beatty in the future, all of which was typed up, mimeoed, and sent home on Friday afternoon. Everyone in town seemed to pay attention. By Saturday evening the waitress at the Exchange Club, a hotel built in 1906 and still there today, was giving us free meals. Her kid was one of our students at the high school, and for the first time she knew how he really felt about life in Beatty, his anxiety to get out on his own and move to Vegas counterbalanced with a strong pride in the life his parents were able to make in the desert. Like many people who end up in Beatty, Goldfield, and Tonopah, she and her family weren't exactly sure it was the best place on earth, but by God it was their place, and if you could make it here, you could make it anywhere.

David and Beth stagger out of the minimart, dazed a little by all the activity, and Beth twists her ankle on a low curb she hadn't noticed. She limps around the asphalt lot for a couple of minutes to work it out, and then takes over the wheel so David and I can inflict some serious voyeurism on the Test Site. The last hundred miles into Las Vegas is where we're closest to it, and we're hoping that even though it's a Sunday there will be some activity to watch. We cross traffic and turn left into the stream of tourists, take the second sharp bend at the southern end of town around the Exchange Club, Beatty's only intersection, and Beth is going over 50 before she notices we're still in a 25-mph

The roadside geology is a nightmare of tectonic rock 'n' roll, individual layers c zone. The end of the drive and gravity beckon, and it's with difficulty that she slows down to 40 before the road and the speed limit open up again.

To our right is what has been identified as the largest cyanide leaching pond in the world, sitting below the demolished hills which our atlas identifies as "Gold Center." To our left, the roadside geology is a nightmare of tectonic rock 'n' roll, individual layers of sediments from ancient seabeds thrust up and colliding at every angle for miles. I know of no place else where you can count as many compacted strata as when you drive around Bare Mountain and sink into the Amargosa Desert, a valley which separates Death Valley National Park from the Test Site. At 3:20 we sight snow-covered Mt. Charleston rising roughly fifty miles away. At almost 12,000 feet and the highest point in the Spring Mountains, it's the largest mountain just outside Las Vegas, hosting a ski area on one of its subsidiary flanks, and a severe visual anomaly as we pass the Amargosa Dunes off on the west side of the valley, elevation 2,660 feet. Dune buggies race up the far steep face only to pop up to the top and do a U-turn for the downhill ride, barely visible from here, mechanical insects playing hide-and-seek.

Yucca Mountain is nearly due north of us, and we scan with the binoculars a settlement of white buildings in that direction, wondering if they're connected to the facility. Singled out in 1987 to be the sole site for further investigation as the nation's repository for high-level nuclear waste, and once referred to accidentally but all too accurately by former U.S. Senator Chic Hecht, a bumbling Reaganite conservative, as the "Nevada suppository," Yucca Mountain is currently designed to hold 70,000 tons of buried radioactive material, some of which will remain deadly for at least 10,000 years. Since no human language has ever lasted that long, scientists are somewhat puzzled by how to ensure the security of the site. Everything from signs in digital code to neoprimitive sculptures intended simply to frighten away the curious have been proposed in what may amount to, for all practical purposes, a permanent monument to estrangement.

ediments from ancient seabeds thrust up and colliding at every angle for miles

This is the most extreme juxtaposition imaginable for any landscape on the planet, the constant reinvention of Las Vegas to keep it the single most visited city in the world, while seventy-five miles northwest as the crow flies we're building the largest and most toxic waste site in the history of our species. Such contradictions could only be designed in a landscape where we can't imagine the consequences, where we have no ostensible use for anything other than its most obvious attribute, emptiness. The town of Beatty will boom once more when the repository opens in 2010 at an estimated cost of $6.6 billion, this time to serve not the extraction of minerals, but the reburying of them.

We've been driving along the border of Nellis for almost two hours at speeds from 70 to 90 mph, and we're not yet at the end of it. The Test Site alone is the size of Rhode Island, and Nellis the parent base about as big as Connecticut, or almost as large as some small countries, such as Israel. Yet it's only now that we begin to see much in the way of buildings, all of which are painted white in a futile attempt to beat back the brutal summer heat. We pass Lathrop Wells, the first entrance for the Test Site: water towers, a paved air-strip, what looks like a graveyard for discarded vehicles, the occasional guard post, and, in the distance, the town of Mercury. The road widens to become the four lanes necessary for the safe commute of workers on their way to Yucca Mountain. There's no identifying the buildings from the highway, but everything from nuclear rocket engines to the railroad system for the mobile MX missiles has been tested out here, and Mercury is the prime control center of the activity. David and I take turns with the binoculars, and I feel that famil-iar flush of embarrassment creeping up my cheeks as I peer over the fence.

About three miles down the road and just prior to the main entrance to Mercury, we pass the semiseasonal Peace Camp, its teepees and tents clus-tered around a small oasis where an intermittent stream flows out of the Spring Mountains. A dozen or so people dressed in traditional rendezvous clothing, those fringed leather replicas of mid-nineteenth-century trappers, are milling around in what appears to be a festive mood. As we get closer to

Las Vegas, it seems only natural that citizens dressed in archaic costumes would be camped across from our preparations for the apocalyptic waste of the twenty-first century.

The road crosses out of Nye and into Clark County, which also marks the start of a small "Desert National Wildlife Area," one of several such located on test ranges throughout the West. While bombing, both conventional and nuclear, literally flattens large hills and fractures the valleys, the off-limit military preserves have also created safe zones for tortoises and antelope, bighorn sheep and rare lizards, animals that have proven perhaps more resilient to dust-borne Alpha particles on the Test Site than weekend recreational off-road vehicle traffic in the Mojave National Preserve.

As we come up to Indian Springs, an auxiliary air force base built to serve the Test Site and the last town before Las Vegas, I tell Beth and David about stopping here one time as several helicopters disgorged a series of high-ranking officers into military vehicles, all of which once loaded promptly sped off into the desert. As if to underline my point, several large Sikorsky airships thrump off to our left. There's a constant line of structures visible now, from concrete blockhouses to viewing stands and observation towers; several large complexes nestle behind some seriously ugly fencing. At first I can't tell what the small dark figures are out on the flats, even with the help of the glasses, and Beth pulls over so we can examine more carefully what looks to be two dozen vehicles advancing in formation across the dry lake bed. David is able to make out tanks, armored personnel carriers, and mobile rocket launchers maneuvering toward each other, a bizarre traffic parallel to the public highway.

The juxtapositions keep coming: the high-security Cold Creek Correctional Facility sits on high ground above a wildlife viewing area, a territory visible to the guards in their towers, and I wonder if they use the high-power surveillance equipment to track the visiting waterfowl. Likewise to the east across the highway, the Floyd Lamb State Park contains verifiable remains of human occupation during the late Pleistocene 11,000 years ago; to the west the living room windows of the modest houses on the Las Vegas Paiute Indian Reservation look out over both the archeological sites and the approaching streets of the city.

Just before five o'clock in the afternoon we find ourselves climbing up a long slow swell in the land that, for a moment, discloses nothing but the clean line of a distant horizon; then, passing under the first overpass since Sparks, we simultaneously cross the city limit and the top of the Stratosphere Tower comes into view, as if it had been planned that way by the Las Vegas Convention and Visitors Authority.

SEVEN

4:35 P.M.: Las Vegas Once again we've survived the day-long journey into Las Vegas. The Painted Desert Golf Course sits to our right, the sprawling Santa Fe Casino to our left, the eighteen-hole greensward mislocated from Arizona and the casino's architecture not resembling in the slightest anything in New Mexico. This is, however, Las Vegas; the point here is not that a casino resemble reality, but rather our image of reality as massaged through thousands of hours of television and movies. To the west and the setting sun lie hundreds of acres of what at first looks to be the red bedrock of the Calico Basin, but upon our closer and astonished inspection is a sea of red tile roofs flowing across the desert and lapping at the foot of the sandstone cliffs. The seam between city and land, between a fantasy of the good life and the reality of a desert where we don't even know how to survive, is invisible. It's there, though, a hairline crack that we cannot bridge just at the edge between the concrete slab supporting the backyard wall and the inward tilt of the Great Basin.

All I wanted to do was find a way gainfully to occupy my time while driving from Santa Fe to Las Vegas, but when I set out on that drive in December 1995 I started a much longer trip than I had anticipated. Twenty-six months and some 6,000 miles later, I finish the thought started on Interstate 25 while crossing beneath an overpass and counting "one." It's the driving, not the road, that wants to be a story, I thought. It's not just about where the road goes, or the two points strung out at either end of the road and a length of time. And it's not just about the relief at leaving and the anticipation of arriving. It's also about how we've literally and metaphorically constructed the road as a view of the world.

Halfway through that first drive I began to realize how difficult our main roads, the interstates, make it for us to read or envision their story. The road and its officially sanctioned attractions, such as parks and fast-gas-food pit stops, are designed to move us along with as little disruption as possible. That's fine for getting from one end of the timeline to another, but flattens our perspective in both visual and emotional fields. In taking conscious note of the road as it exists in its surroundings, I discovered how satisfying it was to jump out of the future tense and the view ahead, instead looking around to both sides and into memories of past experiences. This brings forward the past into the present where it now coexists with the future, that road ahead. Now the linear narrative becomes a synchronous speculation; everything becomes meaningful and connected. As a result, I've probably ruined my ability to get anywhere without thinking about how I'm doing it and how my route has been calculated by others before me. My mania for counting road events has, I'm afraid, increased and even affected my friends and traveling companions, most notably my wife.

The first drive from Santa Fe to Los Angeles found me "pre-" occupied with the nature of landscape, and how we've been trained by art to construct it visually, to modify the land to our needs. We call such needs "taste," as if they were arbitrary aesthetic matters, but they're not. How we view landscape determines how we construct roads across it, which in turn dictates how we view the landscape, a closed circle of perception reinforcing itself from generation to generation.

In America, for example, we convinced ourselves in the nineteenth century that the West was an empty land that needed conquering in order to become useful, the complete subjugation of nature to the needs of man supposedly the destiny of our civilization. So we measured it off in a supposedly democratic square grid, built our railroads and highways, and then designed interstate freeways across it that were as progressively straight as the evolving technology would allow us. We got to the point where we could pretty much ignore the topography of the land and level a passage right through the mountains and across the desert. What few curves were left, in comparison with earlier roads, were there to save time and money in construction and maintenance. We then float along these roads, feeling as if we're the masters of the universe, able to bend the world to our every desire, as if that were our rightful place in the scheme of things. Such confirmation breeds more roads. The road thus is both shaped by and shapes our relationship with the land, which we have modified in the creation of a landscape.

After finishing "Selected Overpasses," the first chapter of this book, I moved on to a number of other writing projects, most of them centered around this issue of how we transform land into landscape. I finished a book about artists working in Nevada, all of whom had specific relationships with the Great Basin, wrote exhibition catalog essays about landscape painting and photography, and gave lectures about cartography in the desert, partly in preparation for a future book on the subject.

In the meantime, I kept driving across the West on roads that began to reveal themselves increasingly through that compounding of attention afforded by counting. Moving from Santa Fe to Los Angeles in the fall of 1996, and attempting to establish a sense of self in a city seemingly devoted to frustrating history, led to another stage in the thought: How do we use the road as a place to exercise memory, and what role does architecture play in those memories? That, in turn, led me directly to consider the construction of fantasy.

When beginning to write in preparation for the 1996 Thanksgiving trip from Los Angeles to Las Vegas, I realized not only that I was halfway to triangulating a physical location, but also that I was drawing a fix on the end of that thought: in order to navigate through the landscape we need stories. Interstates and their amenities, which are a kind of utilitarian or factual architecture, mitigate against that. Fantasy architecture, whether it's in the houses of L.A. or the casinos of Las Vegas, tells a story, but it's mostly hyperbolic, verging on the cartoon or animated feature. The distance from Disneyland to either the houses above Malibu or the Excalibur on the Las Vegas Strip isn't that far, whether measured in miles or metaphors.

This third trip has provided two examples useful in discussing the alternative, which perhaps smart architects have known all along: fictive or imaginative architecture, designs capable of preserving old stories and proposing new ones in our individual and collective memories. The "Mining Machine" at the Silver Legacy was an example of fantasy that failed. Based on genuine historical antecedents of the region, it nevertheless neither adhered enough to the reality to be a scaled-up model, and therefore a traditional "curiosity"—nor did it go far enough in the other direction, fulfilling the promise of being what we understand to be a desirable fantasy at the end of the twentieth century, which is to say a ride at Disneyland. Despite the marketing department's attempt to create a myth about the machine, there's no "place" in the place, hence no "story" in the story.

The Stremmel house doesn't start from such a different premise, the truck stop being another piece of factual, industrial vernacular—but it's made manifest through art, which is premised on enriching the lives of the people around it, not distracting them with an extractive process. The proplike mining gizmo is a half-hearted attempt alluding to a story, where the Stremmel house *is* a story. It's demanding, and therefore not boring; it adds to our understanding of the environment by making us think about it, unlike reinforcing a boring stereotype.

In a parallel sense, the road from Reno isn't as sanitized as the interstates from Santa Fe and Los Angeles. U.S. 95 doesn't separate us physically and emotionally from the environment as much as do the extra lanes, or the ultra symmetry of constant-radius curves and the removal of extraneous junk from the shoulders of the journey, all attributes of the larger roads. It hasn't leveled the landscape before it, which stands mostly preserved through economic malpractice and the military's need for secrecy. It's a road that presents many stories, a visual history of our expectations broken in the desert, from the growing of alfalfa made possible only through federal subsidies, to the massive depredations of mining and the arrogance of the military toward what it is they are supposed to protect, a homeland. Nevada has been called a national sacrifice area, but it simply presents in naked form for all travelers to see what is present elsewhere. The strip mines of West Virginia are mostly hidden from drivers by thick foliage. The military on the East Coast mostly practices offshore, noticed only when they disturb a passenger jet. And the fields in Texas and Oklahoma haven't yet sucked dry the aquifer. But they will. In that sense the desert is an indicator region, where our interactions with the environment show up sooner rather than later.

5:09 P.M.: Henderson We've crossed town, successfully beating out what rush hour there might be on Sunday, and pull off onto the Horizon Drive exit with yet another story for Robert and Polly Beckmann. Two Nevada Highway Patrol guys, both in large four-wheel-drive vehicles, are parked in the dirt, on the horizon if you will, pointing downhill at the direction from which we've come, waiting to catch someone just a little too eager to get downtown. It's the venus-flytrap mentality of Las Vegas. The moving walkways at Caesar's only move one way, into the casino, and you're on your own getting out. The cops don't care about those of us who are leaving, only those who are entering. We loop behind them on the overpass.

Aftermath

Monday, February 17

I hadn't planned on driving to New York–New York, but Beth and David insisted. At least we didn't have to go last night, Robert and Polly quite rightly insisting that we wouldn't be able to see anything through the weekend crowds. It's busy enough this morning at 10 A.M. After circling two of the parking floors without luck, we drove up to the roof to find a space, which turns out not only to have a great view of the backside of the set, so to speak, but also is almost within touching distance of the roller coaster which surrounds the hotel-casino. David envisions stunt people in action movies jumping onto the track to grapple with the bad guys, a wonderfully circular use of the property here, inspired as it is not by reality, but by a New York we know only in cinema.

Taking an elevator down to the third floor, we walk through a skyway and into the video arcade, which is better than anything the casino is likely to offer. Two kids are seated at side-by-side screens as big as garage doors, jockeying animated combatants on the edge of a dizzying precipice, the life-size graphics so detailed the scene compels instant nausea. On the other side an overweight guy in plaid shorts has stepped onto two foot pads and is throwing his torso left and right as he negotiates a virtual downhill ski course. When he crashes the crowd of onlookers actually winces, and he steps out of the experience with sweat on his forehead. Loud popping noises from one aisle over lead us to a more traditional shooting range, where kids are aiming lasers into the mouths of roaring animals in order to win stuffed toys. Teenage employees, sounding as if they'd been coached by watching old movies, hawk the attractions almost, but not quite, like hardened carnies.

The positioning of the arcade is critical, designed to peel off the kids before the escalator takes the parents down to the main floor of the casino, its 84,000 square feet cleverly partitioned from full view by the over-story of fake trees. Unlike descending into the sin-laden atmosphere at Caesar's with its decadent Roman trappings, or the less expensive and no-frills smoky haze of the old-time joints, we ride down into a twinkling Central Park that just happens to have slot machines behind the bushes. The noise level down here is slightly less than that in the arcade, and shifted to a deeper, more serious part of the register. Although it's hard to estimate the size of the crowd, given the carefully designed procession of visual spaces, thousands of people are rotating counterclockwise past the stores and restaurants decorated to represent real locations in New York. This is definitely a major raise in the bidding war over customers on the Strip, an attraction pulling in 200,000 people on opening day a few weeks ago.

We join the flow, which David turns into a sightseeing tour, finding quite accurate the snippets from the New York Public Library, the Stock Exchange, and other monuments recognizable from his days in the city as a cabbie. He pauses to decode the graffiti on a mailbox, dividing the scrawls into those he thinks are authentic and those bogus. I crane my head around to parse the lighting design. The ceiling is miles away, an architectural enhancement made possible by advances in security technology. Instead of the dreaded "eye in the sky" I knew at Harold's Club, which consisted of guys creeping quietly along in the ceilings with binoculars in hand, photographing us through the smoked plexiglass hemispheres embedded over our heads, now

Las Vegas is on a one-way rocket ride where the illusions must become

centrally controlled minicams and computer monitoring of the games has woven security much more pervasively, yet less obtrusively, throughout the casinos.

We take a break outside, first walking over the scaled-down Brooklyn Bridge, then turning back to visit the 150-foot Statue of Liberty which is being sprayed by fire hoses from harbor boats. The spray drifts over us while zooming just behind the verdigris torch at over 65 mph is a roller coaster car full of screaming tourists. New York–New York cost over $460 million to build. The luxurious Bellagio under construction a couple of blocks north is estimated now to ring in at over $1.35 billion, a figure that keeps creeping upward to no one's apparent concern. Venice, Paris, Tahiti, New Orleans, and Rio are cities all being evoked during the nineties in Las Vegas, a city that is becoming a one-stop collection of international entertainments larger than anything Disney could imagine in Florida. While two-thirds of the visitors to Atlantic City go there with the express purpose of gambling in mind, only 13 percent of tourists in Las Vegas arrive with that as their primary reason. Most of the people we're watching this morning aren't throwing down dice; they're gawking and buying trinkets.

Las Vegas has transformed itself into the most fervid destination resort market in the world, another one of those desert superlatives, and it's accomplished this by simply blowing up its past as it goes—the Sands, the Dunes, the Landmark, the Hacienda, all imploded for the ongoing reinvention. And truly, there is no looking back. Las Vegas is on a one-way rocket ride where the illusions must become ever more elaborate in order to keep the customers returning, and all of it will cost more and more until they figure out virtual gambling in cyberspace, which is what the youngsters upstairs are being groomed to inherit. The marketplace drives the technology in response to the

ever more elaborate in order to keep the customers returning.

rising costs of blockbuster fantasies, and the forthcoming shakeout of multiple gaming corporations into three or four giants dominating the table will see to it that the necessary resources are brought to bear.

Back inside we complete our circuit of the downstairs by wandering through the Soho Village giftshop. Even here the illusion is maintained, and the Guggenheim Museum has a display of goods for sale. Over in another corner Beth picks up a candy taxi cab, which David can't help but admire, while I mull over the varied ranks of chocolate Statues of Liberty awaiting consumption. It strikes me as cannibalism, the city ritually swallowing itself in sacrifice, only to be reborn in a new and hungrier assemblage of fantasies. And that brings me back to Robert Beckmann's *"The Body of a House."*

Painted in 1993, the eight large canvases depict a progression of still frames from a movie made on the Test Site in 1953. "Annie" was a sixteen-kiloton shot witnessed not only by 15 million television viewers in a rare broadcast of an atomic test, but also by my parents, who saw the predawn flare of the blast from our hillside home above San Diego. The purpose of the test was to ascertain the effects of such an explosion upon various kinds of shelters, which ranged from simple trenches 2,000 yards away from ground zero filled with crouching soldiers, to a couple of "doomtown" houses, two-story wooden frame homes complete with stocked refrigerators and mannequins arrayed in typical household poses. Robert's paintings depict in microseconds the closer house being dismantled by the blast, a horrifying sequence of iodine-hued images that was first shown in Reno at the Nevada Museum of Art in the fall of 1993. They've been in demand and on tour throughout the country ever since, and are booked for several years in advance.

This isn't a coincidence, that elaborate illusions are constructed in the Great Basin only to be blown up. Las Vegas and the Test Site are next to each other because it's only in the desert that our imaginations will let us get away with such extravagant follies. Only in the largest, emptiest, most desolate place in America could we conceive of letting loose our energies on this scale, whether it's unleashing our largest explosions or our most costly greed, and Robert's paintings of the Test Site are directly pertinent to the nature of Las Vegas.

Gambling is overall a spiral of economic cannibalism—increasingly larger amounts of money eat up smaller ones, concentrating wealth upward from a huge and growing base of customers to the minuscule financial elite of the owners. Money thus migrates mostly from those who need it to those who don't, and while some of it gets reinvested in building still more casinos, the jobs it creates pay so poorly that the employees feel that gambling is their only way out. There's a systemic resemblance to the Cold War, a period when the defense industries of America and the Soviet Union, which constantly had to expand in order to stay alive, magnified a relatively imaginary threat to each other into the genuine possibility of a worldwide apocalypse. The more weapons they built on both sides of the Atlantic, the greater grew the perceived threat, and defense budgets accelerated upwards. The Cold War was a gamble and the growth of gambling is now a series of strategic bluffs in the financial markets. I have no trouble imagining New York–New York being sucked inwards by carefully placed charges when its time comes, and find it only logical that one of Robert's murals is inside.

Once again on top of the garage, the wind has picked up and dark clouds are gathered up north over the Test Site. Each of the three trips I've driven into Las Vegas has had weather, or at least the threat of it, which in this arid city is unusual and hard not to take as a personal portent. They still have flash floods on the Strip, the engineers never having quite figured out how to handle the balance between paving over large amounts of the desert floor and the immense runoff of the thunderstorms, which has nowhere else to flow but down the streets.

We drop David at a car rental place near the airport; he'll stay a couple of days to try the poker games here, seeing if he can improve his luck. Beth redistributes our load in the back seat, and volunteers to drive into Baker for lunch at the Mad Greek. Passing over the state line, I realize I've only opened up more questions about the conversion of land into landscape than I've answered. I repeat to myself: writers write in order to think what they think; writing is the road; traveling on the road is one way of thinking my way into places. It's a circular train of thought and, obviously, I'll have to drive for a while longer in order to straighten it out, thinking up the landscape as I go, a not unhappy prospect.

Selected Sources

The sources listed were consulted by the author during the writing of these essays, are sometimes alluded to in the text, and may be of interest to readers.

As general background

Nash, Gerald D. *Creating the West: Historical Interpretations 1890–1990.* Albuquerque: University of New Mexico Press, 1991.

Ryden, Kent C. *Mapping the Invisible Landscape: Folklore, Writing, and the Sense of Place.* Iowa City: University of Iowa Press, 1993.

Solnit, Rebecca. *Savage Dreams: A Journey into the Hidden Wars of the American West.* San Francisco: Sierra Club Books, 1994.

Stegner, Wallace. *The American West as Living Space.* Ann Arbor: University of Michigan Press, 1987.

Turner, Frederick. *Beyond Geography.* New York: Viking Penguin, 1980.

Wilson, Alexander. *The Culture of Nature: North American Landscape from Disney to the Exxon Valdez.* Cambridge, Mass.: Blackwell Publishers, 1992.

Worster, Donald. *Rivers of Empire.* New York: Random House, 1985.

——. *Under Western Skies: Nature and History in the American West.* New York: Oxford University Press, 1992.

Basin and Range/Great Basin/Nevada

Castleman, Deke. *Nevada Handbook, 4th ed.* Chico, Calif.: Moon Publications, 1995. One of the few general guidebooks to the state, each successive edition has become more complete, the most recent of which was especially invaluable in writing about the Reno–Las Vegas drive.

Fiero, Bill. *Geology of the Great Basin.* Reno: University of Nevada Press, 1986.

Grayson, Donald K. *The Desert's Past: A Natural Prehistory of the Great Basin.* Washington, D.C.: Smithsonian Institution Press, 1993. The most comprehensive overview of the Great Basin.

Hess, Alan. *Viva Las Vegas: After-Hours Architecture.* San Francisco: Chronicle Books, 1993. A succinct, compelling, and essential book about the history of architecture in "the ultimate disposable city," lavishly illustrated as only Chronicle knows how.

Houghton, Samuel G. *A Trace of Desert Waters: The Great Basin Story.* Reno: University of Nevada Press, 1994. Originally published in 1976, this remains the definitive study of water in the Great Basin, and is also a valuable compendium regarding the history, natural and otherwise, of this desert.

Hunt, Charles B. *Natural Regions of the United States and Canada.* San Francisco: W. H. Freeman and Company, 1974.

McPhee, John. *Basin and Range.* New York: Farrar, Straus, Giroux, 1981.

Ronald, Ann. "Why don't they write about Nevada?" In *Wilderness Tapestry,* edited by Samuel I. Zeveloff, L. Mikel Vause, and William H. McVaugh. Reno: University of Nevada Press, 1992.

——.*Earthtones: A Nevada Album.* Reno: University of Nevada Press, 1995.

Shepperson, Wilbur, ed. *East of Eden, West of Zion.* Reno: University of Nevada Press, 1989.

——.*Mirage-Land: Images of Nevada.* Reno: University of Nevada Press, 1992. A history of language as applied to the state from John C. Frémont to Jean Baudrillard.

Tronnes, Mike, ed. *Literary Las Vegas: The Best Writing About America's Most Fabulous City.* New York: Henry Holt and Company, 1995.

Trimble, Steven. *The Sagebrush Ocean: A Natural History of the Great Basin.* Reno: University of Nevada Press, 1989.

Selected Overpasses

Beardsley, John. *Earthworks and Beyond.* New York: Abbeville Press, 1989.

Brown, Julia, ed. *Michael Heizer: Sculpture in Reverse.* Los Angeles: Museum of Contemporary Art, 1984.

——.*Occluded Front: James Turrell.* Larkspur Landing, Calif.: Lapis Press, 1985. Overview of Turrell's career.

Chilton, Lance, et al. *New Mexico: A New Guide to the Colorful State.* Albuquerque: University of New Mexico Press, 1984.

Chronic, Halka. *Roadside Geology of New Mexico.* Missoula, Mont.: Mountains Press Publishing Company, 1987.

Heizer, Michael. *Double Negative: Sculpture in the Land.* New York: Rizzoli, 1991.

Mitchell, W. J. T., ed. *Landscape and Power.* Chicago: University of Chicago Press, 1994.

Novak, Barbara. *Nature and Culture.* New York: Oxford University Press, 1980. Landscape, art, religion, and science in nineteenth-century America.

Sonfist, Alan, ed. *Art in the Land: A Critical Anthology of Environmental Art.* New York: E. P. Dutton, 1983.

Turrell, James. *Mapping Spaces: A Topographic Survey of the Work.* New York: Peter Blum Editions, 1987.

Counting Backwards

Bachelard, Gaston. *The Poetics of Space.* Boston: Beacon Press, 1994. Despite the title, this much cited text deals mostly with interior and intimate spaces, but nonetheless contains clues about our conceptions of distance in landscape.

Berger, K. T. *Where the Road and the Sky Collide: America Through the Eyes of Its Drivers.* New York: Henry Holt and Company, 1993

Banham, Reyner. *Los Angeles: The Architecture of Four Ecologies.* New York: Penguin Books, 1990. Originally published in 1971, this affectionate overview of the built environment in L.A. makes it the essential counterpart to Venturi's study of Las Vegas published a year later.

——. *Scenes in America Deserta.* Layton, Utah: Gibbs M. Smith, 1982. Banham was a self-confessed "desert freak," as fond of the desert east of Los Angeles as of the city. Required inoculation against the Baudrillard cited below.

Baudrillard, Jean. *America.* Translated by Chris Turner. London: Verso, 1988. Despite Baudrillard's statement that he knows the American deserts better than Americans, a claim belied by the numerous errors of fact contained in this book, he is living proof of how media images have molded our perception of the desert landscape, and how those images, if not the land itself, have created an architecture of fantasy and simulation.

Bengston, Jeff, et al. *Playing It Safe: A Players's Guide to Crime Prevention.* Las Vegas, Nev.: Bengston-Scott Publishing, 1993.

Darlington, David. *The Mojave: A Portrait of the Definitive American Desert.* New York: Henry Holt and Company, 1996. Required as an antidote to the above cited Baudrillard.

Davis, Mike. *City of Quartz: Excavating the Future in Los Angeles.* New York: Vintage Books, 1992.

Dewey, Fred. "Letter from Freedom X: Baudrillard Does Vegas." *Coagula Art Journal* 25 (January 1997): 46–50.

Eco, Umberto. "Travels in Hyperreality." In *Travels in Hyperreality: Essays.* Translated by William Weaver. New York: Harcourt Brace Jovanovich, 1986. The title essay by this Italian has become one of the touchstones in American cultural criticism, dealing as it does with our construction of various architectural fantasies as manifestations of our individual and collective psyches. As with Banham and Theroux, the observations of the chronic outsider are unique.

Knight, Christopher. *Last Chance for Eden: Selected Art Criticism by Christopher Knight 1979–1994.* Los Angeles: Art Issues Press, 1995. Edited by Malin Wilson with a foreword by Dave Hickey, this wide-ranging collection of Knight's pieces for the "*Los Angeles Times*" is essential reading for those investigating the cultural milieu of L.A. The quote regarding desire is from page 337 in his 1990 piece titled "Is L.A. a World-Class Art City?"

Krist, John. *Fifty Best Short Hikes in California Deserts: In and Around Death Valley, Joshua Tree and Mojave.* Berkeley: Wilderness Press, 1995.

McNamee, Gregory, ed. *The Sierra Club Desert Reader.* San Francisco: Sierra Club Books, 1995.

McPhee, John. "Los Angeles Against the Mountains." In *The Control of Nature.* New York: Farrar, Straus, Giroux, 1989. Ostensibly about L.A.'s struggle to contain erosion on its northern edge, as always McPhee provides more cogent information about the larger subject, in this case the urban hubris of L.A., than almost anyone else.

Ovnick, Merry. *Los Angeles: The End of the Rainbow.* Los Angeles: Balcony Press, 1994. Excellent social history of architecture in Los Angeles, profusely illustrated with photographs by Carol Monteverde.

Schwartz, Gary. "*Ars Moriendi:* The Mortality of Art." *Art in America* 84, no. 11 (December 1996). This is a succinct and statistically compelling examination of how we base our ideas of progress in art, if not in civilization, on the false notion that we save the best from the past.

Scott, Allen J., and Edward W. Soja, eds. *The City: Los Angeles and Urban Theory at the End of the Twentieth Century.* Berkeley: University of California Press, 1996. Fourteen indispensable essays on Los Angeles and all it portends for the rest of the world; topics range from architecture to transportation policy.

Spanier, David. *Welcome to the Pleasuredome: Inside Las Vegas.* Reno: University of Nevada Press, 1992. Of particular interest is Chapter 4, "Signs and Wonders," which gives a succinct overview of prevailing attitudes regarding the architecture of Las Vegas and the place of signs within it.

Theroux, Peter. *Translating L.A. : A Tour of the Rainbow City.* New York: W. W. Norton, 1994. Theroux tours the city by car and public transportation as a translator both linguistic and cultural.

Venturi, Robert, Denise Scott Brown, Steven Izenour. *Learning from Las Vegas.* Cambridge, Mass.: MIT Press, 1977. This 1972 study, revised only five years later and re-released in a more affordable edition, turned American architectural studies on its head, and is quoted by almost everyone who writes about Las Vegas.

The information regarding archeology at the Calico Early Man Site was informed by two articles in particular:

Powledge, Tabitha M., and Mark Rose. "The Great DNA Hunt, Part II: Colonizing the Americas." *Archaeology* 49, no. 6 (November/December 1996): 58–68.

Lavick, Roy, and Russell L. Ciochon. "The African Emergence and Early Asian Dispersals of the Genus *Homo*." *American Scientist* 84, no. 6 (November/December 1996): 538–51.

The *Los Angeles Times* remains one of the great research tools about the contemporary American West. Articles quoted or alluded to in this essay include:

Clifford, Frank. "Can the Mojave Survive?" *Los Angeles Times,* December 11, 1996, 1, 16–17.

Gardetta, Dave. "The Strip: Something's Happening Here, What It Is Ain't Exactly Clear." *Los Angeles Times Magazine,* December 15, 1996, 24–67.

O'Neill, Ann W. "You'd Be Surprised What a Mere $10 Million Can Get You These Days." *Los Angeles Times Magazine,* December 8, 1966, 16–54.

Swed, Mark. "Hundreds, by Design, Weigh Role of Chance." *Los Angeles Times,* November 11, A1, A24.

What Counts

Much of the information regarding casino construction and the state of Nevada's economy was culled from the *Reno Gazette–Journal* and forwarded to me by Jim McCormick during December 1996 and January 1997; Robert and Polly Beckmann provided a similar clipping service for material from the *Las Vegas Review–Journal* during the same period.

Basso, Keith. *Wisdom Sits in Places.* Albuquerque: University of New Mexico Press, 1996. A readable and important ethnographic study of how the Apache language is used to link place, memory, stories, and wisdom. Despite the specificity of the subject matter, it provides insights relevant and accessible to us all.

Fox, William. *Mapping the Empty: Eight Artists in the Great Basin.* Reno: University of Nevada Press, 1998. This collection of essays contains a more complete description of Robert Beckmann and his work, as well as that of Michael Heizer and other artists dealing with the region.

Land, Barbara, and Myrick Land. *A Short History of Reno*. Reno: University of Nevada Press, 1995.

Schjeldahl, Peter. "Helluva Town." *Art issues* 46 (January/February): 14–19. A humorous and sharp take on Las Vegas in general, and New York–New York in particular by the art critic for the *"Village Voice."*

Short, Gary. *Flying Over Sonny Liston*. Reno: University of Nevada Press, 1996.

172

I would especially like to thank Matthew Coolidge at the Center for Land Use Interpretation (WWW:http:/clui.zone.org/clui.html or 310–839–5722) for his help in locating information about the munitions depot in Hawthorne. The center has also published *The Nevada Test Site: A Guide to America's Proving Ground* (1996), which is of great interest.